A POST-TRIBULATION MANIFESTO

BREAKING THE PRE- AND MID-TRIBULATION RAPTURE *SPELL*

Jon Eric Lambert

New Harbor Press
Rapid City, SD

Copyright © 2025 Jon Eric Lambert

All rights reserved. No part of this publication may be reproduced, distributed or transmitted in any form or by any means, including photocopying, recording, or other electronic or mechanical methods, without the prior written permission of the publisher, except in the case of brief quotations embodied in critical reviews and certain other non-commercial uses permitted by copyright law. For permission requests, write to the publisher, addressed "Attention: Permissions Coordinator," at the address below.

New Harbor Press

1601 Mt Rushmore Rd, Ste 3288

Rapid City, SD 57701

www.newharborpress.com

Ordering Information:

Quantity sales. Special discounts are available on quantity purchases by corporations, associations, and others. For details, contact the "Special Sales Department" at the address above.

A Post-Tribulation Manifesto/Lambert —1st ed.

Scriptures taken from the Holy Bible, New International Version®, NIV®. Copyright © 1973, 1978, 1984, 2011 by Biblica, Inc.™ Used by permission of Zondervan. All rights reserved worldwide. www.zondervan.com The "NIV" and "New International Version" are trademarks registered in the United States Patent and Trademark Office by Biblica, Inc.™

ISBN 978-1-63357-462-5

First edition: 10 9 8 7 6 5 4 3 2 1

Contents

To the Church in America, a letter of concern: 1

Introduction 5

The Interpretation of Scripture 7

A Wrench in the Smooth Argument 13

When the Watchman Blows his Trumpet 17

Where Does the Bible Teach the Post-tribulation Rapture? 19

Where does Jesus teach the Order of Resurrection? 25

Could Jesus Come at any Moment? 33

The Timing of our Relief from Persecution 49

Second Thessalonians 1 & 2 53

Is It True That the Church is Not Mentioned From Chapter 4 to the End of Revelation? 61

When and Then 63

The Argument That We Are Exempt from Wrath 67

The Time of Trial 73

A Poignant Conclusion 75

The Devastation False Promises Cause—The Sudden Distress of the Church in the Tribulation 79

Worthy of the Kingdom of God 83

The Watchman's Duty 89

Two Commands to the Church 91

An Afterword: Here Are Some Things We Can Do 93

What All Three Views of the Rapture Can Do Together 95

Your Perfect Life in America is Not The Life of
Millions of Christians 97

Hastening the Day 99

Post Script 109

To the Church in America, a Letter of Concern:

The Issue

The church is divided into hostile camps. This division is not between believers and non-believers inside the church, but between genuine believers in Christ who hold different views of the timing of the Rapture, the timing of the gathering of the saints to Jesus, *vis-à-vie* His Second Coming.

Some may be unaware of the intensity of the disagreement among these three views of the rapture. This is likely because one of the three is not on the receiving end of the hostility shown to divergent views. The majority opinion knowingly or unknowingly afflicts those with minority opinions.

Also, I am concerned that those who hold the majority opinion are completely mistaken and promising things Jesus did not promise. In particular, I see disaster coming to the church in America because of the pre- or mid-tribulation rapture theologies. This is my personal concern—though I cannot find anyone else that will rouse themselves to react to it, or even see a problem. But it is a huge problem in these end-times.

The Puzzle

It is strange that the church clings to something nowhere taught in Scripture. It has become the classic story of the emperor having no clothes. In this particular case, however, participants are not coddling up to the king to curry favor and thereby not perceiving his nakedness, but rather they cannot perceive this nakedness from a sincere desire to love and respect their pastor and what he preaches. They will study it no further than what they are taught from the pulpit and find no need to; they are content not to consider it any further. The pre-tribulation rapture embraces them like a python.

The challenge to you is to find a clear proclamation of Scripture that shows a pre- or mid-tribulation rapture *that is not some kind of inference, or assumption, or reference to cultural Jewish wedding practices, or using typology to make its case* in lieu of the literal method of interpreting Scripture. Inferred evidence is **nothing**; what we need to find are unequivocal references in the Word of God.

Lot being rescued from Sodom or Noah being rescued in a boat before the Flood is inferred evidence that the rapture of the church must be before the Tribulation. When compared to **crystal clear** statements that the church will be rescued from persecution at the end of the Tribulation, these inferences mean little.

In the course of writing this manifesto, I watched a YouTube video of a well-known Bible scholar who passed away some years ago. He breathlessly referenced Jewish wedding practices, typology, and a doctrine of imminency (meaning: Jesus could come at any time) to try to prove his case for the pre-tribulation rapture. However, he referenced *not a single verse* of Scripture other than these inferences that "proved" his point. He declared other views of the timing of the rapture to be deficient, because they denied the doctrine of imminency.

As you will see, there is no such "doctrine of imminency" in Scripture to deny. He made slanderous inuendoes against those who hold a different view as if they would not be "pure" by holding an opposing view, and he threw in a couple of jokes that insulted anyone of a different opinion. He made the untrue claim that those who held other views were not literalists—yet offered no verses for us to interpret literally. It is easy to argue your case from a podium when no one else from the other side is there to challenge what you say.

But to laugh out of the church and slander those who honestly disagree with the pre-tribulation rapture and who can prove their viewpoint with unequivocal passages from Scripture, borders on not loving the brothers. This is a very serious offense against Christ. Something is wrong.

At the end of this manifesto is a call for significant, biblical cooperation among these three opposing views. This cooperation is on common ground that all sides of the divide can agree to. Prepare to be saddened and amazed.

In Christ,

Jon Eric Lambert
Chaplain, Major
US Army, Retired

Preparation for study: Read Matthew 24, Mark 13, Luke 17:20-37 and Luke 21:5-36, 1 Thessalonians 4:13-5:11, 2 Thessalonians 1:5-12 and 2:1-12, Revelation 16:15 and its context.

Introduction

The Tribulation itself is seven years long, and the Great Tribulation is the latter half of that; it is 3½ years long. Scripture tells us in four different ways so we could not mistake it: half of seven—3½ years, 42 months—3½ years, 1260 days—3½ lunar years, and a time, times [a double word], and a half of time. These all indicate 3½ years.

Some denominations to this day refuse to see the plain meaning of the text and think this repetition means nothing. They do not talk about it, nor do they study it. Yet, as far back as 1844, it was generally agreed that the time periods of 42 months and 1,260 days and a year, two years and a half year were synonymous periods of time and all of these were equal to three and a half years (*Thoughts on a Spiritual Understanding of the Apocalypse, or the Book of Revelation*, Leavitt, Trow & Co., Publishers).

However, belief in a literal Tribulation, no matter how you slice it, is no longer shared by all denominations. That is a broader subject and beyond the purpose of this book. However, all Christians should be interested in Daniel's prophecy of the first coming of Christ. It uses a time sequence and is very precise. The time period of the Tribulation (the rest of Daniel's prophecy) is also precise.

The topic is not as arcane as it may seem at first, and we are given scriptural tools to figure it out—it is not difficult. Daniel was given a prophecy of the coming of the Messiah with a specific chronology.

Since Judah had disobeyed God and had not rested its land in the Sabbath year for 490 years, they were expelled from the land of Israel, based on the time formula given to Israel in Leviticus 26:34-35. Because of the multiplied sins of Israel, the people would be removed from the land, but the length of time for this removal was based on every year the land wasn't rested in its Sabbath year. At the close of 2 Chronicles the chroniclers specifically mentioned the literal fulfillment of Leviticus 26 and the prophecy of Jeremiah that the land would lie desolate for 70 years (2 Chronicles 36:21, Jeremiah 25:11).

Four hundred ninety years divided by seven (every seventh year was a Sabbath year) is 70—so this would be the length of Judah's banishment from the land. At the end of this time period, Daniel was reading and in prayer about Jeremiah's prophecy that the exile would be 70 years long (Daniel 9:2-3). As he was praying about this, he was interrupted by the angel Gabriel who declared a similar 490 years (seventy sevens) prophecy. It is a remarkable prophecy that shows when the Messiah Himself should first appear (see Alva J. McClain's *Daniel's Prophecy of the 70 Weeks*).

That the Tribulation itself is seven years is plainly seen from Daniel's seventy sevens prophecy (Daniel 9:24-27). The first 69 sevens were consummated at the cutting off (the death) of the Messiah, Jesus' first coming. The final seven has yet to occur, based on Jesus' reference to the antichrist in His Olivet discourse (Matthew 24:15), based on Paul's reference to the antichrist many years later (2 Thessalonians 2:3), and at the end of the first century, John's reference in Revelation (13:5).

This manifesto is about that final seven years and how church theology is divided over the timing of the rapture and the Second Coming of Christ. Our aim is to explore the correct, though neglected, post-tribulation view. At the end of this brief manifesto, there is a call for cooperative action concerning two major Bible prophecies that will hasten the day of Christ. On this, all three views can agree.

The Interpretation of Scripture

The pre-tribulation rapture of the church is taught in many Bible-believing churches. This teaching means that the church will leave the earth *before* the seven-year Tribulation. Its teaching warns us to be saved so that we will not be "left behind" to suffer the events of the Tribulation.

In spite of this, and to its credit, many (though not all) who hold the pre-tribulation view have stopped teaching that Matthew 24:40 means the rapture even though "*left behind*" was a popular Christian song lyric and the title of a Christian film series.

> Two men will be in the field; one will be *taken* and the other *left*. (Emphasis added)

However, it has since been recognized that this is not a verse that shows a pre-tribulation rapture, because the parallel in the passage is "the flood *took* them all away." This is not a rescue, but rather a taking away to judgment as Luke 17:35-37 clarifies further:

> Two women will be grinding grain together; one will be *taken* and the other left. 'Where Lord?' they asked. He replied, 'Where there is a dead body, there the *vultures* will gather.' (Emphasis added. Wuest—"the birds that feed on putrefied flesh."—The New Testament, An Expanded Version, Eerdmans)

This reminds us of Revelation 19:17,18—

> And I saw an angel standing in the sun, who cried in a loud voice to all the birds flying in midair, 'Come gather together for the great supper of God so that you may eat the flesh of kings, generals, and mighty men, of horses and their riders, and the flesh of all people, free and slave, small and great.'

This event surrounds the Second Coming of Jesus.

> He treads the winepress of the fury of the wrath of God Almighty.

And, He is the—

> King of kings and Lord of lords. (Revelation 19:15,16).

On the other hand, this entire discussion is considered unimportant by some saints. And others flatly refuse to discuss it. It is very important to them to *believe* that the pre-tribulation rapture is true; for them it is important to maintain harmony at all costs and at the expense of discussing Scripture. For a few, the details of Scripture give them a headache—why study it? However, Scripture *should* hold sway for us all, because it is an important part of the whole counsel of God.

Some refuse to discuss it, because for them controversy of any kind in the church is to be avoided. Yet, to refrain from discussion leaves in place discrimination against brothers and sisters in Christ, because imminency and the pre-tribulation rapture are still prominent in their doctrinal statements though these are stunningly unproven contentions. Agreeing to these propositions are mandatory to be able to serve in these churches.

Despite those who don't want controversy of any kind, Paul taught these things to very young-in-the-Lord believers anyway. So, why should we hesitate to dive in? To hesitate is the second part of the *spell* that has been cast over the church.

To say that a *spell* has been cast over the church is a startling way to put it. *Spell* is a strong word. So, another less harsh way to put it is to compare it to the power of a traditional view of Scripture. These may be precious teachings to us whether or not they are taught in Scripture and whether or not the Scripture might contradict them—many times we cling to them anyway.

For instance, let's say that your church takes a stand on some issue of doctrine contrary to another denomination. Either side may or may not be correct. There might be a friendly chat or earnest debate between you and the other side, but when the other believer points out a clear verse of Scripture that plainly contradicts your denomination's point of view—it may expose a painful weakness in your argument.

One book that argued its denominational stand cited what Scripture said in one column labeled "What the Bible Says" (meaning the point of view of their church) and the second column it was labeled "What Baptists say". This method was meant to argue against the major antagonists of that denomination, namely Baptists. The one who showed me the book pointed out a particular doctrine where the Bible supposedly contradicted the Baptists.

In the first column, the cited passage of Scripture claimed the waters of baptism were absolutely necessary for salvation. Baptist doctrine in the second column indicated that the waters of baptism are not what saves a Christian. To clarify the discussion, I looked up the Scripture the book had cited and read the full text.

The Bible was actually misquoted in the first column. As it turned out, the book had quoted part of the verse, placing a period part of the way through and left out the part of the verse that said it was not the water that saved a person but rather a pledge of a good conscience toward God (1 Peter 3:21)!

Misquoting Scripture does not an argument make—their tradition had trumped the plain text of the Bible. They were willing to misquote the Bible to prove their point that you must be baptized or you cannot be saved. [Believers should be baptized, but Peter points out that the water which removes dirt from the body is not what saves.]

In another but separate example, Scripture says Jesus had siblings (Mark 3:31-32). This contradicts the doctrine that says Mary was a perpetual virgin. Rather, the truth according to Scripture was that Jesus was born supernaturally to Mary the virgin, and then He was followed by other children that Joseph and Mary had together in the natural way—

> But [Joseph] had no union with her *until* she gave birth to a son. (Matthew 1:25, emphasis added)

After the supernatural birth of Jesus, other children were born to Mary and Joseph as normally would happen with a married couple. These are not "cousins" as some say, nor step-brothers and step-sisters supposedly from Joseph's prior marriage as another branch of Christianity claims. Psalm 69:8 predicts of the Messiah:

> I am a stranger to my brothers, an alien to my own mother's sons.

Rather than this plain Scripture ending the debate, most members of these churches who believe the "Mary was a perpetual virgin" doctrine **double down**, because they are attached to their view, they love their church and their denomination, and they love their pastor or priest. And they are exalting Mary beyond the bounds of Scripture (1 Corinthians 4:6, Paul's admonition, "Do not go beyond what is written.").

Most will probably continue to reject the other side's verses of Scripture (Mark 3:31-32, Psalm 69:8, Matthew 1:25) in spite of the 'knockout punch' they have just received. In a friendly debate, an Eastern Orthodox chaplain merely changed the subject, ignoring Psalm 69. [Also, the logic of Eastern Orthodox theologians on this subject is the most tortured logic you could ever read.]

Besides doubling down, some might even get hot-under-the-collar. They would reject the other side's interpretation of the verses, because they (of course) are on the "right" side of God, et cetera, et cetera. For whatever reason, they fight on.

Changing one's mind and owning the plain meaning of Scripture to the detriment of fondly held views is painful. Nobody likes to admit they were wrong, and nobody likes a painful reversing of a viewpoint, much less trying to drag their fellow denominationalists into adopting this new point of view. So, instead of changing our opinions, we fight on—or ignore the controversy—as silly as either of these may sound. After all, we believe the Bible is supposed to guide us in our faith and to be on our side; it is not supposed to lead us to views that we have never held before!

It is actually an important point of character to admit when you are wrong. This should happen, however, only when the Scriptures convince and compel you—in spite of fondly held traditions.

There is a popular, secular song of yester-year by the "Primitive Radio Gods" that seems to accuse Christians of believing that God always sides with their opinions. For honest souls this is astonishingly untrue! On the other hand, traditionally held views normally make most Christians surprisingly hard-headed. *Spells* do the same! (See Revelation 18:23.)

Spell is a strong word, but I do not think of myself as a particularly smart person. I grieve, however, when I see those under this spell say things to their own harm that don't come from Scripture and even contradict it! Perhaps as you read this manifesto you will grieve with me too.

A Wrench in the Smooth Argument

The major views divide into three categories: the coming of Jesus for the church before the seven-year Tribulation—called the pre-tribulation rapture; a mid-tribulation rapture—a coming for the church in the middle of the seven-year Tribulation at the three and a half year-mark; or Jesus comes for the church at the end of the seven-year Tribulation—a post-tribulation rapture.

Bible colleges many times teach the pretribulation rapture as absolute fact. They are so certain of this truth that they have been known not to graduate anyone who believes otherwise. But God catches the wise in their craftiness (Job 5:13).

My Bible college used the textbook *Things to Come* for eschatology, the study of what the Bible has to say about the end-times. Confident that this book would satisfy the challenge of a debate that I had entered into (fifty-some years ago), I eagerly looked up every verse cited about the rapture in order to argue the Bible only taught a pre-tribulation rapture and that our Bible professors obviously knew what they were talking about.

The arguments presented in the book, however, were vanishingly weak. The verses did not say what the author implied they said—except that it fell into the trap of circular reasoning, and confirmation bias. There were no verses that declared a pre-tribulation rapture, which for me indicated the emperor was wearing no clothes. I was laughed at for my temerity in questioning the guru-above-all-gurus on the subject of the pre-tribulation rapture. I hadn't even graduated from Bible college and had the hutzpah to disagree with this prestigious author.

Finding that the emperor had no clothes was jarring. The pre-tribulation rapture was the only doctrine that I had ever been taught. I loved my Bible college and I loved its professors. I was *defending* the pre-tribulation argument but finding my legs cut out from under me. However, I was young enough to change my view of the rapture before I grew too old and set in my ways to have the strength to change.

I had a memorable meeting with our Old Testament professor. He was an extremely likable man, a favorite among the students—godly, humble and very knowledgeable. He politely listened to all my arguments for a post-tribulation rapture and declared in the end that the verses made sense, and the post-tribulation argument was *correct*—the verses did indeed indicate a post-tribulation rapture (!).

However, in the end, he protested this conclusion, because Dispensationalism changed everything when it is overlaid on the text*. This elated and saddened me at the same time. Elated because he had seen the plain meaning of the Bible text. He had agreed with me that a post-tribulation rapture was what Scripture plainly taught.

[*In any case, as I found out, some Dispensationalists do hold a post-tribulation view, so my favorite professor's point was made moot.]

But it saddened at the same time. A system of interpretation no matter how much it is thought to be true must not change—indeed *cannot* change, the plain meaning of the text. And, as has been said of UFOs, "Extraordinary claims must have extraordinary proof." Yet we have no biblical warrant to say we have unequivocal, undisputed proof that Dispensationalism changes the plain meaning of the text. Nor could it change it.

Dispensationalism basically states that a distinction should be made between the church and Israel. Supposedly this distinction grows out of a consistent "normal or plain" interpretation of the text (Ryrie, *Dispensationalism Today*). But what if the Bible says something plainly that contradicts this new system of overlaid theology? Can Scripture be overruled by a system of theology developed in the 19th century (or in any century)? I personally think not...*not at all*.

Dispensationalists have decided that God will not work with different groups and different covenants at the same time. The timing of the prophecy of Daniel's seventy-sevens holds a key for them. As a whole, the prophecy is only for Daniel's people the Jews (Daniel 9:24). Dispensationalists see proof of this in the gap between the 69th seven and the 70th seven. This gap is the church age. The gap in the prophecy started as the prophetic clock stopped ticking with the death and rejection of Israel's Messiah. So, after the pre-tribulation rapture, they say Daniel's clock starts ticking again for the Jewish people—for the final seven years of Daniel's prophecy.

This reasoning is flawed, however, because **by *itself*** it cannot justify a radical view like the pretribulation rapture of the church without clear statements showing that this view of the rapture is true. There are no statements in the New Testament that declare a pre- or mid-tribulation rapture. We ask, why would we be left guessing about the coming of Jesus for us? Why would Jesus fail to mention that the rapture of the church is a different gathering than the one at the end of the Tribulation in Matthew 24?

Inferential reasoning is not good enough to overturn clear statements of Scripture.

Hence, this manifesto is published in order to warn the American church. In particular, it is the American church has been infused with the pre-tribulation rapture theology and to a much lesser extent the mid-tribulation rapture. In my circles, those that believe a post-tribulation rapture are few and far between.

When the Watchman Blows his Trumpet

Some cannot agree with the arguments presented here—but ask yourself at the end of our arguments, why not? Why can't they? I have argued the post-tribulation rapture with friends and (theological) enemies. I have preached it from the pulpit, taught it in Bible studies and argued the case in emails with smart people.

A few have agreed with me on the Scriptures that I cite. But, for the most part, a smothering, all-encompassing, cheerful view has settled over the church in America, and they don't want to think about it further. We cannot just shout that the pre-tribulation rapture must be true and hope for the best—we must produce clear Bible texts that show it.

However, we are reminded of two things: [1] Jeremiah seemed very alone too. Not many converts to his message either. And [2] Not many laymen live and breathe the Scriptures every day.

The point is to be a watchman on the walls and to declare what we *know* to be true. Imagine the chaos when the time of Tribulation manifests. Christians will find that the expected rapture *before* the worst tribulation ever is not taught anywhere in Scripture. *Not at all*. And no one in their churches gave a warning. The warning voices have already been silenced.

It is guaranteed that the pre-tribulation rapture is a false expectation. No use beating around the bush. Sound the alarm and see who listens to the warning.

That our favorite pastors (and our favorite professors of the Bible) have been badly deceived and have taught what is not taught in the Bible is unfortunate, if not **catastrophic**. Let me repeat: there are absolutely no verses that directly and unequivocally teach a pre-tribulation rapture. Not one. Assumptions have to be made first and then inferences must be made from those assumptions in order to support the idea of a pre-tribulation rapture. Circular reasoning abounds.

Yet, there are several unequivocal passages that declare a post-tribulation rapture—no assumptions have to be made first. It would take a powerful *spell* cast upon a believer to make him (or her) miss these obvious Scriptures.

Since the Tribulation is the worst persecution that the church will ever see—never to experience the like again (Matthew 24:21)—shouldn't the church be warned? *Shouldn't there be a clear-eyed discussion of what we are facing?*

Where Does the Bible Teach the Post-tribulation Rapture?

As if Matthew 24 is proclaiming the emperor has no clothes, the text is very plain—Jesus is very plain: the rapture of the church is "*after* the distress of those days." Jesus clearly says He will come with the clouds of heaven, with the shout of the archangel and the great blast of the trumpet of God to gather His *elect*—*after* the distress of those days (24:29).

Who does Jesus gather after the distress of those days? The *elect*—and on this the issue of the timing of the rapture is decided. We find there are three opinions on the meaning of *elect* in Matthew 24. Which view we pick makes all the difference in our interpretation—but our selection of which definition of *elect* is the right one must be according to truth, not preference.

1. Some believe Jesus is gathering *elect* Tribulation saints who have survived to the end. They are not the church, the bride of Christ, but rather those who were not raptured earlier. This version of the *elect* says they are those who belatedly come to faith in Christ and are raptured at the end of the seven-year Tribulation.
2. Many believe that Jesus means He is gathering *elect* Jews at His second coming. For Dispensationalists, it is the Jewish nation that is gathered at the end of the Tribulation when Jesus returns.

3. Some believe that Jesus is specifically referring to the gathering of His *elect* church, the bride of Christ, at the end the Great Tribulation.

The first view (#1) is not correct for several glaring reasons.

a. If this gathering of Tribulation saints was exclusively for them and not for the church itself—then we must ask, where does Jesus speak of a pre-tribulation gathering of His beloved church in Matthew 24? Our gathering is left out entirely. He makes no mention of our gathering—not before the Tribulation, not in the middle of the Tribulation, nor at the end of the Tribulation. Not a peep. That's like a description of a wedding and leaving out the bride!

Also,

b. This view (and the next view, #2) fails to take into account how the apostles looked at the word elect in the rest of the New Testament: the same Greek word is used over and over again to describe the church. (1) and (2) both fail to notice how Paul looks at Matthew 24 and how he used it to describe the rapture of the church. This is a *catastrophic* oversight for both the first and second views of who the *elect* are. More on this in the next section.

The second view (#2) sees certain Jewish features referred to in the passage, and therefore, it declares the church is not meant by the term *elect*, but rather Israel is meant.

These Jewish features are—

> ...then let those who are in *Judea* flee to the mountains... (Matthew 24:16, emphasis added)

And

> Pray that your flight will not take place in winter or on the **Sabbath**. (Matthew 24:20, emphasis added)

I believe these indicators do address those living in Israel at the time of the Tribulation—but Jesus' audience on the Mount of Olives was His disciples—representatives of His fledgling church, not representatives of the nation of Israel. A key factor in Bible interpretation is "audience." We ask, then, who was Jesus' audience in Matthew 24, and how would they interpret what was being said?

We also notice that the antichrist will enter the rebuilt Temple (Matthew 24:15) and that Jerusalem will be the epicenter of the persecution. *Of course* this is in *Judea*. And anyone in Israel who flees on a **Sabbath** at that time will stand out from the rest. This is especially true at a time when Israel will become a very religious country.

With services restarted in the newly rebuilt Temple, Sabbath-keeping will be much more intense during those days. Any long-distance movement on a Sabbath would stand out like a sore thumb. Jesus would not need to give a similar warning anywhere else in the world. The warning is pertinent to Jewish Christians and Gentile Christians in Jerusalem at the center of the coming storm. Jewish and Gentile Christians, not unbelieving Jews, will be familiar with Jesus' words when the end-times come.

Further, and in connection to "audience" and in contradiction to the view that *elect* means the nation of Israel, the term *elect** was specifically used several chapters before Matthew 24 and used *in particular* of those who believe in Christ. It was also used there in *counter-distinction* to the nation of Israel—those who do not believe Jesus is the Christ (Matthew 22:2-14). Then, in context and by word-usage, *elect* is firmly established to mean the church.

> For many are invited, but few are **chosen***. (Matthew 22:14, emphasis added)

And,

> He is Lord of lords and King of kings—and with him will be his called, **chosen*** and faithful followers. (Revelation 17:14, emphasis added. *The Greek is the same in all three Scriptures.)

The disciples who listened to Jesus on the Mount of Olives knew that He meant the church was His *elect* and only believers in Jesus. Jesus was telling His apostolic audience, as representatives of His church, what they could expect before His coming. This is more than obvious.

To say that the disciples were Jewish and therefore represented the Jewish nation in this passage (as opposed to the soon-to-be-leaders of the Christian church) is wishful thinking that has an obvious agenda—a predetermined but misguided outcome to the debate.

Also, and even more precisely, the second view (#2) is incorrect, because the Old Testament's description of the gathering of the Jews at the end of the age shows that it will be done in a totally mundane way. According to Old Testament prophecy, Israel will be gathered by the peoples of earth on horses, chariots, wagons, mules, and camels—not supernaturally by angels (Isaiah 66:20).

> For with fire and with his sword the LORD will execute judgment upon all men, and many will be those slain by the LORD ... 'And they will bring all your brothers, to my holy mountain in Jerusalem as an offering to the LORD—on horses, in chariots and wagons, and on mules and camels,' says the LORD. (Isaiah 66:16, 20)

[I mentioned this passage to a doctor of theology recently and though it plainly undermined his view of who the **elect** are in Matthew—he **doubled down** and denied it.]

So, not only is the church's gathering to Christ left out of the narrative of Matthew 24 in the pre-tribulation rapture view, but also a false "gathering of the Jews" or even a false narrative of "Tribulation saints" has supplanted it.

In the third view (#3), His faithful followers, His **elect**, His church will be gathered by angels in a supernatural way—not by people, not on donkeys, oxcarts, or whatever—but rather by angels—supernaturally.

The third view is the natural reading of the passage. It is not a welcome, inviting view because of all the horrors of the Tribulation that have been taught in American churches in the context of preaching the pre-tribulation rapture. And it is not what has been emphatically declared by Bible-believing pastors. Yet there it is—not only a sound interpretation of the text, and the only viable interpretation, but one completely worthy of consideration—not ridicule.

With the decisive elimination of views (#1) and (#2), the post-tribulation rapture of the church is plainly seen here. Jesus said it clearly—He is coming for us *after* the events of the Tribulation. With these verses in mind, read the text carefully and you will see that the church is being warned—not Israel.

Unfortunately, some have declared, "Pray for pre, Prepare for post." In this way, we can believe what we want to believe without any challenge or messy debates. Of course this avoids confrontation, but it also avoids the necessary discussion. Putting our heads in the sand does not an argument make.

Perhaps Jeremiah should have taught both views of the coming of the Babylonians— "Some say the Babylonians are coming, but Some say they are not!" In this way, he could be approved of as a cheerful prophet of God (because he was nice and reasonable) and people could choose which view they liked best! But

God demanded that Jeremiah confront Israel. God is appalled by ***double-speak***. In the end, Jeremiah insulted those who said the Babylonians were not coming. He was jailed and almost killed for it.

Where does Jesus teach the Order of Resurrection?

This answers how the apostles viewed Jesus' message in Matthew 24.

I assume that many do not know the answer to the question *Where does Jesus teach the order of resurrection*? I concluded this after a survey went to many of those who had attended my Bible college over the years and to several former professors—93 in all viewed the question. Another query went out to numerous acquaintances and friends of mine. Of the 93 who read the question, and of all the friends asked, not one of them answered. However, the answer is critical. It establishes for us Paul's use of Jesus' earthly teaching.

Paul wrote that his teaching on our subject was *"according to the Lord's own word"* (NIV) or *"by the word of the Lord* (KJV)." By the authority of this word, he gave the order of the resurrection—the gathering of deceased and living saints. (1 Thessalonians 4:15).

> *According to the Lord's own word*, we tell you that we who are still alive, who are left till the coming of the Lord, will certainly not precede those who have fallen asleep. For the Lord himself will come down from heaven, with a loud command, with the voice of the archangel and with the trumpet call of God, and the dead in Christ will rise first. After that, we who are still alive and are left will

> be caught up together with them in the clouds to meet the Lord in the air. (1 Thessalonians 4:15-17, emphasis added)

By what **word** did Jesus teach this order of resurrection? Where in the Gospels did Jesus teach this? Or, on the other hand, was "*according to the Lord's own word*" a reference to special revelation that Paul got straight from Jesus Himself?

Many would attribute "*the Lord's own word*" to a teaching that Paul received privately by revelation. On the other hand, as we read the Gospel of John and the resurrection of Lazarus (chapter 11:17ff), there is a sudden realization that Paul had before him the same passage (or he had in mind Lazarus's story straight from the apostles themselves). When he gave his assurance that the dead in Christ would be raised first, it was from this very passage and by the authority of Jesus Himself.

In John 11, Jesus taught Martha the meaning of the resurrection and its order. Martha, Jesus' friend and disciple, was very upset with Jesus for staying away from Bethany after He had been told that her brother, and Jesus' friend, was very ill. Lazarus had been so ill that he died and was in the tomb four days by the time Jesus finally showed up.

It is true, on the other hand, that Martha's anger at Jesus was mixed with her respect for Him as her miracle-working Master. She softened her rebuke by saying "even now I know that God will give you whatever you ask" (John 11:22).

Jesus countered Martha's statement with "Your brother will rise again." Yet, Martha's rebuttal was both blunt and informed: "*I know* he will rise at the resurrection on the *last day!*" [Read Martha's statement with sharp, indignant passion.]

Jesus had certainly taught that there would be a resurrection on the *last day* (John 6:39-40). She was repeating this teaching to Him as if she knew very well that her brother would rise on the *last day*—but *that* was not her point. His refusal to come quickly to rescue her sick brother was the issue—not a future resurrection on the *last day*.

Jesus (mildly) corrected her view of the resurrection—it was not just a *day* in the future—the Resurrection was Jesus *Himself*!

He then gave the order of resurrection that Paul cites. Yet, when we read this in isolation, it seems incomprehensible:

> Jesus said to her, 'I am the resurrection and the life. He who believes in me will live, even though he dies; and whoever lives and believes in me will never die. Do you believe this?' (John 11:25-26)

Yes, Lazarus fit the first scenario—Believe-die-live again on the *last day*, but he did not fit the second part—Live-believe-never die. My former conclusion: Jesus must have meant that a believer never really dies. You could call this a *spiritualized* view, because with this you could believe what Jesus said to Martha to the best of your ability. Otherwise, to take Jesus literally would mean that He contradicted Himself!

It does seem contradictory outside of the context of Paul's letter to the Thessalonians. Believe-die-live again *but also*, Live-believe-never die. The meaning is not self-evident in isolation; Lazarus had obviously believed in Jesus but died anyway. But Paul picked up on something we would likely have missed.

Let's back up a bit. Jesus' sayings as well as copies of the Gospels and Apostolic letters to the churches were in circulation during the time of Paul's ministry. Paul asked Timothy to:

> Bring the cloak that I left with Carpus at Troas, and my scrolls, especially the parchments. (2 Timothy 4:13)

We also see James (the brother of Jesus) repeat the teachings of Jesus from the Sermon on the Mount (Matthew 5-7) in all five chapters of his book. And we see Peter referring to Paul's writings as Scripture—so he obviously had seen copies of Paul's letters:

> Just as our dear brother Paul also wrote you with the wisdom God gave him...His letters contain some things that are hard to understand, which ignorant and unstable people distort, as they do the other *Scriptures*, to their own destruction. (2 Peter 3:15-16, emphasis added)

The circulation of the teachings of Jesus and the sharing of precious documents was of utmost importance to the early church. Paul's letters were to be read by other churches:

> After this letter has been read to you, see that it is also read in the church of the Laodiceans and that you in turn read the letter from Laodicea. (Colossians 4:16)

John wrote on a scroll *what he had seen, what is now, and what will take place later* and sent it to the seven churches in Asia Minor, circulating the scroll to each church—the one message to all the churches being sent round-a-bout in a scroll to all seven (Revelation 1:11,19).

1 Corinthians 7 is another example of Paul referring to the teachings of Jesus while He was with us on earth. In this passage, Paul cited Jesus separately from his own apostolic teaching:

> To the married I give this command (not I, **but the Lord**): A wife must not separate from her husband. (1 Corinthians 7:10, emphasis added)

This matches the strict rules Jesus laid down in Matthew 5:32 and 19:6,9.

Then Paul added his own advice, because new situations had arisen in the early church. Paul had to add new teaching, because some had come to believe in Jesus but their husbands or their wives had not yet come to believe.

> To the rest I say this (**I,** not the Lord): If any brother has a wife who is not a believer and she is willing to live with him, he must not divorce her. (1 Corinthians 7:12, emphasis added)

This situation had to be ruled on, since in the Old Testament, the remnant Jews who had returned from exile were forced to divorce their foreign, unbelieving wives they had married outside the community of faith (Nehemiah 13:23-28 and Ezra 9 and 10). This was such an egregious sin and violation of the law of Moses that some Jews and even some priests had committed, that to make things right, they had to divorce their foreign wives and send them away.

A judgment had to be made in each of these cases in Nehemiah's time, because, of course, the Israelites had the exceptions of Ruth the Moabitess and Rahab the innkeeper from Jericho to consider. These women were converts to Judaism as would also have been the case with some of the wives in Nehemiah and Ezra's day. They too might have converted to Judaism and so divorce would not be necessary.

The early church's situation was different for the most part, since no one is born into the Christian faith as the people of Israel are born into Judaism. Rather, people come to believe in Jesus later in life, and they are born-again by choice and by faith. But they may have already been married when they came to faith in Jesus. Paul says the reason for a believer to stay with their unbelieving wife or unbelieving husband is for the children's sake and to hope for their partner's salvation (1 Corinthians 7:12-14).

Paul the Apostle distinguished his teaching from the Master Himself: "not I, but *the Lord*" and "*I*, not the Lord."

So, it is reasonable to assume that Paul knew the story of Lazarus well and saw Jesus clearly teaching the order of resurrection. This was a very great comfort to the Thessalonians who had thought their deceased loved ones had missed out on the coming of Jesus. Don't worry, he explained to them, the dead in Christ will rise first. How could they know this for certain? Jesus Himself had taught it—it was *the Lord's own word*—not Paul's word, but *the Lord's*.

With this in mind, Paul was not only citing Jesus' teaching, using it in 1 Thessalonians 4:15 about the order of resurrection, but also citing *another* direct teaching of Jesus and this one about the rapture of the church. This word of the Lord was—

> At that time the sign of *the Son of Man* will appear *in the sky*, and all the nations of the earth will mourn. They will see the Son of Man coming on the *clouds of the sky*, with power and great glory. And he will send his angels with a *loud trumpet call*, and they will gather his elect from the four winds, from one end of the heavens to the other. (Matthew 24:30-31, emphasis added)

Paul was referencing the story of Lazarus's resurrection (John 11), which was Jesus' teaching on the order of resurrection, and *in the same verses*, Paul was referencing Matthew 24 (details of the rapture) in order to show that his teaching had great, direct authority: "by the word of the Lord," meaning Christ's teaching while on earth—not I, but the LORD Himself.

Again, Paul wrote—

> "*According to the Lord's own word*, we tell you that we who are still alive, who are left till the coming

of the Lord, will certainly not precede those who have fallen asleep. For *the Lord himself* will come down from *heaven*, with a *loud command*, with the voice of the archangel and with *the trumpet call of God*, and the dead will rise first. After that, we who are still alive and are left will be *caught up with them* in the clouds to meet the Lord in the air. And so, we will be with the Lord *forever*. (1Thessalonians 4:15-17, emphasis added)

There are definite, unmistakable parallels:

John 11, "***Jesus said*** to her,…"
1 Thessalonians 4, "According to the **Lord's own word**…"

John 11, "He who believes in me **will live**, even though he **dies**…'"
1 Thessalonians 4, "the **dead will rise** first."

John 11, "whoever **lives** and believes in me will **never die**…"
1 Thessalonians 4, "we who are **still alive** … and so we will be with the Lord ***forever***."

Matthew 24, "They will see the **Son of Man coming**…"
1 Thessalonians 4, "the **Lord himself will come** down"

Matthew 24, "on the ***clouds*** of the sky…"
1 Thessalonians 4, "from heaven…in the ***clouds***"

Matthew 24, "his ***angels*** with a loud ***trumpet call***…"
1 Thess. 4, "voice of the ***archangel*** and with the ***trumpet call*** of God"

Matthew 24, "they will ***gather*** his elect…"
1 Thessalonians 4, "we will be ***caught up*** with them"

We would be hard pressed to find another event that Paul would be referencing with this kind of language. One could only willfully not see these parallels.

Thus, we see the order of resurrection from John 11, and the rapture of the church from Matthew 24, and these are both ***according to the Lord's own word.***

I would hazard a guess that many mature Christians would not know that Paul was actually citing Jesus' own word to Martha about the order of resurrection and Jesus' own word on the rapture. Certainly, pre-tribulation theologians have missed it. Without a presupposed agenda, it is obvious that Paul was citing the teachings of Jesus on His coming for the church. We can be certain of this.

Could Jesus Come at any Moment?

A major contention of the pre-tribulation world-view is that Jesus could come at any moment with no predicted events preceding it. If that were true, then we would have to ignore (with difficulty) the conclusions of the above arguments.

And, if it is true that there are no events that must occur before His secret coming, then a post-tribulation rapture is out of the question. A post-tribulation rapture of necessity must be preceded by many signs and events. The pre-tribulation view says there are no events coming on the prophetic calendar that need to be fulfilled before His secret coming—His coming is sudden and wholly unexpected. But saying so, does not make it so.

The pre-tribulation view presupposes that His coming is secret and sudden and therefore unannounced. But there are no verses that say His coming is anything other than He is **revealed**, His coming is **loud**, His coming is with **blazing fire**, and His coming is with **powerful angels** at His side.

There are several reasons why the 'imminent coming of Jesus' argument is made against the post-tribulation view. The pre-tribulation argument claims that the coming of Jesus is imminent (He could come at any moment), based on the fact that Jesus said "**no man knows**" the time of His coming. You must therefore be ready for the coming of the Master at any and all times. He will come at a time that you will not expect Him—like a thief in the night (Matthew 24:42-44).

Yet, we can all agree that the passing of time does not allow for a change in the original intent of Scripture. In other words, if Jesus said that Peter would die as an old man (John 21:18), any pronouncement of Jesus *before* the old age death of Peter would not change its meaning or interpretation *after* the death of Peter.

He could not have returned at any time *before* Peter died in his old age—or even in Peter's younger years before he grew old. So, whatever Jesus said about His thief-like coming *cannot* mean what we may assume it might mean.

Similarly, "this gospel of the kingdom will be preached in the whole world as a testimony to all nations, and then the end will come" (Matthew 24:14). This calls for a *very* long wait before Jesus returns. The end could not come until the Good News of the Kingdom would be preached in every corner of the world.

Therefore, His coming has not been imminent for nearly two thousand years. The passage of time cannot change the meaning of Jesus' words. Jesus could not have been teaching that imminency was true at all times and in every circumstance —for the very reason that His two predictions had not happened yet. The one required decades before Peter would become an old man and the other required a long, long period of missionary work (millennia) before the consummation of the age.

Besides this, Jesus Himself directly warned the people that His coming would certainly be after a long time:

> While they were listening to this, he went on to tell them a parable, because he was near Jerusalem and the people thought that the kingdom was going to appear *at once*. He said: 'A man of noble birth went to a ***distant country*** to have himself appointed king and then to return.' (Luke 19:11-12, emphasis added)

His parable was specifically to tamp down the notion that the kingdom was to come *at once*. The nobleman must first go to a *distant country* (implying a long journey). A similar point was made in Matthew 25:14ff and here the language implies a long wait: *"after a long time the Master of those servants returned"* (vs 19).

We may be excused for taking this to mean a long indefinite time, as He plainly means: *"a man of noble birth went to a distant country"* and *"after a long time the master of those servants returned."* By these two alone, no one could say that the kingdom was going to appear at once, but rather, it would appear after a long time.

Jesus warned the disciples that they personally would *not see* the days of the Son of Man:

> Then he said to his disciples, 'The time is coming when you will long to see one of the days of the Son of Man, *but you will not see it.* Men will tell you, *"There he is!"* or *"Here he is!"* Do not go running off after them. For the Son of Man in his day will be like the lightning, which flashes and lights up the sky from one end to the other. But first he must suffer many things and be rejected by this generation.' (Luke 17:22-25, emphasis added)

It is also true that this passage is in the context of a question by the Pharisees about the timing of the arrival of the kingdom. Right enough, Jesus said that the kingdom would not come visibly so that people could say, *"Here it is!"* or *"There it is!"* and then He added "because the kingdom of God is *within* you" (Luke 17:21). But as Wuest correctly captures the meaning, "the kingdom of God is in your *midst*" (Wuest, The New Testament, An Expanded Translation, Eerdmans). This is the principle that the presence of the King means the presence of the Kingdom.

Jesus meant that when the King is with them, or in their midst, they are in the Kingdom—in other words, it is nothing to be observed over there or over here apart from Jesus Himself. Along these same lines, Jesus made an odd comment that some of His disciples would not die before they saw the Son of Man coming in His kingdom (Matthew 16:28) even though He had earlier said they **would not see it**.

Since His kingdom supposedly did not manifest while Jesus was on the earth, liberal interpreters conclude that Jesus Himself was mistaken about when the kingdom would come (!). Odd that those in the church would deny their Master's deity (see below).

Again, context tells all. Matthew 16:28 is followed immediately by the story of the transfiguration recorded in Matthew 17:1-13. In other words, Peter, James and John did see the Son of Man coming in His kingdom, because they saw the Son of Man glorified. The presence of the King means the presence of the Kingdom. The Pharisees could not declare, "Here it is!" or "There it is!" because they failed to see that Jesus was the King, and He was already in their midst.

Even so, after the resurrection, the disciples' excitement could not be contained when they asked Him, "Lord, are you at this time going to restore the kingdom to Israel?" (Acts 1:6). They had forgotten all His tamping down of expectations and His teaching that He would be away a *long time* and that they **would not see His day**. He reminded them that the good news of the kingdom had to be preached all over the world first.

The teaching of the thief-like coming of Jesus is tricky unless it is taken as a whole. But this thief-like coming doesn't mean what most teach for three reasons: **[1]** Both Jesus and Paul say that believers will **not be surprised** by this thief-like coming and **[2]** We have missed **the intended target** of Jesus' message and **[3] The thief-like coming of Jesus is repeated** at the end of Revelation's judgements **at the battle of Armageddon**.

When we tell each other in excited, knowing tones that Jesus might return before the church service has ended (as I once did and many still do) and what a beautiful surprise it would be (because no man knows the day or the hour of His coming) we are forgetting that Paul said the following.

> But you, brothers, are not in darkness so that this day should surprise you *like a thief.* You are all sons of the light and sons of the day. We do not belong to the night or to the darkness. So then, let us not be like others, who are asleep, but let us be alert and self-controlled. For those who *sleep, sleep* at night, and those who get *drunk, get drunk* at night. (1 Thessalonians 5:4-7, emphasis added; parallel references to *sleepers* as in Revelation 3:3 and *drunkards*, Matthew 24:49.)

[1] Not surprised

Congregations of believers have sons of the light/sons of the day—and on the other hand, congregations also have those who *fall asleep* when they should be watching for Jesus. They *get drunk* and beat their fellow servants. These church-goers will indeed be surprised (but in a bad way) and the rest will not be surprised—pleased and excited, watching and waiting—but not surprised like a thief coming in the night. As Jesus illustrated in Matthew 24:48-50—

> But suppose that servant is *wicked* and says to himself, 'My master is staying away *a long time,*' and he then begins to beat his fellow servants and to eat and drink with *drunkards.* The master of that servant will come on a day when he does not expect him and at an hour he is not aware of. (Emphasis added)

In the space of two chapters Jesus claimed He would return after *a long time*—in Matthew 24:48 and in Matthew 25:19. This long delay actually leads some in the church to act wickedly and to deny His coming—but Jesus Himself gave us this warning.

The only ones who would be surprised are **wicked** congregants who are pretend- Christians—pretend-believers. They are not true believers as Luke 12:45-46 explains—

> The master of that servant will come on a day when he does not expect him and at an hour he is not aware of. He will cut him to pieces and assign him a place with the **unbelievers**. (Emphasis added)

The charade will end badly for drunken church leaders and church-going hypocrites, but those watching and waiting will not be surprised.

[2] *The intended target of Jesus' message*

At this point, Peter spoke up and wanted to know exactly to whom Jesus was telling His parable—was it "to us or ***to everyone***?" (Luke 12:41, emphasis added).

The answer Peter got was the story of the faithful and wise manager. If that servant was found doing what his master wanted when the Master returned—he would be rewarded. On the other hand, there will be those who are not true believers, and they *will be* surprised by His coming. They are hypocrites and theirs is the place of weeping and gnashing of teeth (Matthew 24:51).

So, in the Gospel of Luke (12:40), Jesus said, "You also must be ready, because the Son of Man will come at an hour when ***you*** do not expect him", followed by the question from Peter. However, Jesus' answer in the Gospel of Luke to the question Peter asks, "are you telling this parable to us or to everyone?' *was a story—**not** a direct answer.*

On the other hand, in Mark's gospel, it was a direct answer, but Peter's question was not recorded—

> Therefore keep watch because you do not know when the owner of the house will come back—whether in the evening, or at midnight, or when the rooster crows, or at dawn. If he comes suddenly, do not let him find you sleeping. What I say *to you*, I say *to everyone*: 'Watch!' (Mark 13:35-37, emphasis added)

The message was directed *to the disciples* and *to everyone*—both the true believers and the fake believers who attend church. Rather than telling individuals to decide for themselves whether or not they are on the awake side or the asleep side, Jesus told *them* and tells *everyone* in His household to watch. And His message had the intended effect—the true church has been faithfully watching for nearly 2,000 years, being alert and staying awake. If He comes suddenly, those disciples who are awake would not be surprised, but the asleep members of the church would indeed be surprised—but in a bad way.

Jesus' message will be heeded by true believers. If you are believing His word—watching, expecting, and doing what the Master has assigned to His servants when He returns—believing in Jesus and loving the brothers (1 John 3:23)—then you can certainly expect to be rewarded by the Master.

By the same understanding, the wicked in the church are being given a chance to *wake up*. But if the wicked have stopped watching and start ridiculing others for waiting for the coming of Jesus, putting up roadblocks for others to come to faith, then they can expect to be treated like any other unbeliever when Jesus returns.

This has happened before and is happening in the church today. There are chaplains, priests and pastors that are a grievous puzzle. Some think that to be "born-again" is not necessary in order to enter the kingdom of God (even though their Master proclaimed it was). Some commit the sin of idolatry of mixing Baal and the God of Israel together in their rituals. Others don't really believe in the resurrection of Jesus and think that it is not a necessary belief—even though it is the centerpiece of our salvation and of our hope for the resurrection and for our eternal life. These teachings are crucial to our faith (Romans 10:9-10). A dead Jesus is of no use to us (1 Corinthians 15:12-14).

There are cultic off-shoots of the Christian faith that are by no means Christian even though they proclaim that they are. These large groups exist especially in the United States, and they deny the deity of Christ. They will accept no argument that shows the opposite of what they believe in spite of the volumes of passages in Scripture that show that Jesus is indeed God in human flesh. Romans 10:9-10 is once again a critical passage that shows grievous wolves have entered the church and deceived, because they deny His deity and/or deny His bodily resurrection.

The late Catholic pope is an apostate for saying that all religions lead to God. Catholic bishops have also said this—not to mention Protestant ministers. The famous Christmas hymn, *O Come, O Come Emmanuel* has been banned from certain churches in England, because it would be offensive to Jewish people, proclaiming Jesus is their Messiah! Yet, Jesus declares that He is indeed Israel's long awaited Good Shepherd (Ezekiel 34, John 10:9,11,14), and also that He is the only truth—the only way to the Father (John 14:6).

Years ago, two Protestant chaplains advised me to stop preaching the fulfilled prophecies of Christ's first coming. Chapel services were filled with basic trainees, and these two chaplains claimed this preaching might offend Jewish soldiers in the chapel service. Their temerity and ignorance and apostasy were shocking.

First of all, no one is compelled to attend chapel services in any case, and certainly no one is compelled to attend services that are not of their religious choice. Second, no Protestant chaplain in a Protestant chapel service is constrained to accommodate those who do not believe Christian doctrine. Third, these two chaplains were unfaithful to the message of Christ themselves, one having already stopped certain Christ-centered hymn-singing in his service lest a Jewish man who attended his services be offended! [This chaplain was also arrested for lewd crimes several months later after our confrontation.] Legally, morally, professionally, ethically and in loyalty to Christ, these two were dead wrong.

Also, in a chaplains' meeting many years ago, two Catholic priests were joking about priests who were attracted to little boys or attracted to little girls. They were amused at the church's solution. If a priest had a problem with little boys, then he was moved to a girls' school. If he were attracted to little girls, he would be moved to a boys' school. Why weren't these offending priests removed from the priesthood? Oh, they said, once a priest, always a priest! This was not, however, how the priest Martin Luther was treated.

Recently, a member of a particular religious order proclaimed the most outrageous abominations about who our Creator is. He ascribed our creation to aliens from outer space. He declared all religions to be fabrications of aliens—all religions were made up and were meant to shepherd us along in our evolutionary journey.

He also stated that Fundamentalists, Baptists, and others, to include some Catholics, had to change their doctrine in order to accommodate the coming disclosure of alien existence. His organization is working toward effecting this change. Yet, he is a member of his religious order in good standing—the same religious order that the past pope belonged to.

A member of my Baptist church had formerly been involved with a cult while in college. The cult taught that its adherents could participate in any sin they felt like as long as they confessed it later. This person revealed that Catholic nuns in New York City had participated with her in wild revelry. They were involved in the most unbelievable sins.

Are any of these waiting and watching faithfully? No. These are the abusers that Jesus had in mind—they beat their fellow church-goers, lead them astray, and hide their true beliefs and practices from their congregants, and get "***drunk***" in the night.

Jesus knew that the church in all ages would be mixed—some in the church would be true believers, and some would not be. He knew that Christianity would succeed in spreading around the world and that wolves would enter the church, not sparing the flock, causing real havoc.

So, Jesus' message was to the church at large (which includes both believers and unbelievers)—I am coming like a thief in the night, and you won't know when. Yet, Paul assured the church at Thessalonica that they were on the right side of Jesus—being alert, watching and waiting for His coming. They would absolutely *not* be surprised by His thief-like coming.

Imminency could not be a viable doctrine five hundred years ago in the days of the Reformation, since the Gospel of the Kingdom had yet to be preached to all nations. Imminency could not have been taught or true in the first century before Peter became an old man. Jesus' thief-like coming could be longed for and watched for but only with the idea that things had to happen first and that the spread of the Gospel would take ages and ages to fulfill.

The so-called 'doctrine' of the imminent coming of Jesus is not possible, because there were unfulfilled predictions that Jesus had made about the future that would conclude before His coming. These precluded an understanding that Jesus taught He could come at any moment. The meaning of His words would not and could not change to mean something else centuries later.

In addition, Jesus taught that the Kingdom of God would only come when the signs of the Tribulation were at hand—

> Look at the fig tree and all the trees. When they sprout leaves, you can see for yourselves and know that summer is near. Even so, when you see these things happening, you know the kingdom of God is near. (Luke 21:29-31)

This passage in Luke's Gospel is in the context of the seven-year Tribulation. When you see these things happening, you will know that the Kingdom is near. These are definite signs Jesus said we should watch for.

In the middle of the Tribulation, the antichrist will declare himself to be God in the Temple of God. Yet, this was and is *not* an ever-present reality; there has been no Temple in Jerusalem since AD 70 (Matthew 24:15 and 2 Thessalonians 2:4). These are signs of His coming that are very clear but are not universal in all ages—they could only be true at the end of the world.

Because the Temple has not been a reality for nearly 20 centuries, some denominations have decided to spiritualize much of the Bible's predictions about the future. Prophecies about Israel as a nation in the end-times was not a reality from AD 70 to 1948. That tended to make some theologians spiritualize everything.

On the other hand, it wasn't just Paul who said that watchers for Jesus' coming would not be surprised; Jesus Himself said it—

> **Be careful, or** your hearts will be weighed down with dissipation, drunkenness and the anxieties of life, and that day will close on you unexpectedly like a trap. For it will come upon all those who live on the face of the whole earth. Be always on the watch, and pray that you may be able to escape all that is about to happen, and that you

may be able to stand before the Son of Man. (Luke 21:34-36, emphasis added)

Notice at least five things that Jesus affirmed in Luke 21:29-36—

1. We can and will see signs of His coming and these signs are the events of the Tribulation.
2. The Kingdom is still future, we are not in it now.
3. Jesus also stated that the trap of the Day of the Lord would catch some, but true believers could escape the trap by watching and being alert for His coming. The trap would be sprung upon the entire world but would *not* trap those who are *careful* and watching—just as Paul also stated in 1 Thessalonians 5:4.
4. It will come on the whole earth, so we are a part of this story, too.
5. We should pray to escape all these things. [Those of the pre- and mid-tribulation raptures don't have to pray this, because they won't be here for the events of the Tribulation. But then, why did Jesus bother to tell us to pray to escape these things if it were not a possibility to be involved in these events? To whom was He recommending prayer, and how could we ignore Him?]

[3] ***The thief-like coming of Jesus is repeated*** at the end of Revelation's judgements ***at the battle of Armageddon.***

The thief-like coming of Jesus is at the battle of Armageddon at the end of the Tribulation, *according to the* L<small>ORD</small>*'s own word.* Quoting Jesus, John writes—

Behold, I come ***like a thief***! Blessed is he who stays awake and keeps his clothes with him, so that he may not go naked and be shamefully exposed. (Revelation 16:15, emphasis added)

We note the context of "Behold, I come *like a thief*!" is at the end of the Tribulation:

1. This is at the end of the judgement bowls between the 6th and the 7th (Rev. 16:12 &17).
2. It is at the battle of Armageddon.
3. As the seventh bowl is poured out, **lightning**, **rumblings**, peals of **thunder** and an **earthquake** take place the likes of which have never occurred before—and then the King returns (Revelation 19:11ff).

These are the same events ending the trumpets and the seals.

At the sounding of the seventh trumpet: Revelation 11:15 &19—flashes of **lightning**, **rumblings**, peals of **thunder**, an **earthquake** and a great hailstorm.

At the opening of the sixth seal: Revelation 6:12,13,16, and 17—a **great earthquake**, the sun turns black like sackcloth, the whole moon turns blood red, stars fall from the sky, the sky recedes and is rolled up, every island and every mountain is removed from their places, **the great day of the wrath of God and of the Lamb** has come.

[As in Matthew 24:29: tribulation-sun and moon and stars darkened-the revelation of Christ].

In other words, even though these three (bowls, trumpets and seals) may start at different times in the narrative of the book of Revelation, it is a crescendo of judgments that all end at the same time with the same events. The order of events in Revelation must not be linear but each of the judgments (bowls, trumpets and seals) circles back on the timeline—only to end with the same events. So, in context, these show ***the thief-like coming of Jesus** must be* at the end of the Tribulation.

> 4. That the original readers of Revelation would expect the thief-like coming of Jesus at the end the Tribulation comes from the same warning that Jesus had earlier given to the church in Sardis in the same book (Revelation 3:3). It was a familiar warning to them and is also meant to warn us—

> Remember, therefore, what you have received and heard; obey it, and repent. But if you do not wake up, I will come ***like a thief***, and you will not know at what time I will come to you. (Emphasis added)

This means, once again, there are those in the church that need salvation and they need to wake up before it is too late. They needed to repent and believe the Gospel that had been preached over and over again in the church of Sardis. This Gospel has also been preached over and over again in our churches. Take heed; "Today is the day of salvation" before it overcomes us like a thief in the night.

The reverse of this must also be true—If you do wake up you *will* know approximately, because Jesus told us in this context you will know "the kingdom of God is near." You *will* see the signs of the Tribulation—and you will *not* be caught off guard ***like a thief*** coming in the night.

When Jesus taught 2000 years ago that neither He nor the angels knew about the day or the hour and *"no man **knows** about that day or hour"* or *"Therefore keep watch, because you do not **know** on what day your Lord will come,"* we note He used the present tense (Matthew 24:36, 42).

In a similar case of reasoning, when confronted by the Sadducees, it is important to see that Jesus turned His whole argument for the resurrection on the tense of a verb in Matthew 22:32,

> I *am* the God of Abraham, the God of Isaac, and the God of Jacob. (Emphasis added)

This must not escape our notice. The Sadducees should have known that there is a resurrection simply because of the fact that God is not the God of the dead but of the living **based on the tense of a verb.** Similarly, two thousand years ago, Jesus did not know, the angels did not know, no man knew—but at the least, in the future, we certainly think that Jesus *will* know and will not be surprised. We can perceive that His coming is near by the events observed in the Tribulation.

Though in the Gospels *a thief-like* coming was seemingly told as if it were a sudden, unexpected surprise to the church as a whole, the reality is that it would only trap those who are not believers—even though they are in the church.

The *worry* of the true believer is mitigated by a sincere belief that Jesus is our Savior. He has saved us by the promise that "everyone who believes in him may have eternal life" (John 3:15). He is returning for us someday, and we as a church need to be alert. We should be on the watch for Him and for the signs of His coming. Certainly, Paul had great confidence in the church of Thessalonica that they would not be surprised and that was nearly 2,000 years ago.

By these three *[1], [2], and [3]*, the pre-tribulation rapture's understanding of imminency is shown to be false.

There are so many holes in the theory of the imminent return of Christ, it is like a sieve leaking water. So, why do Christians believe it? I can only imagine that they have heard it all their lives—without challenge.

The Timing of our Relief from Persecution

Paul makes it abundantly clear that our rescue from persecution coincides with the awesome, violent Second Coming of Jesus—not with a secret pre- or mid-tribulation rapture.

Paul started his epistle to the Thessalonians, mentioning the church was undergoing persecution at that time (2 Thessalonians 1:4). His comfort to them was in the midst of great suffering, but their suffering was evidence that God's judgment was right. Through these sufferings, they would be *counted worthy of the kingdom of God*.

American Christians *do not* notice that the comfort Paul writes about is the comfort of being *counted worthy of the kingdom of God for which they were suffering* (2 Thessalonians 1:5)—not the comfort of being persecution-free—nor the comfort of a pre-tribulation rapture.

For the most part, American Christians do not expect *any* persecution as if they were somehow exempt. They have been assured over and over and over again that the church will be raptured before the seven-year Tribulation. Could they, will they turn on each other when the time for their testing comes?

> You will be betrayed by parents, brothers, relatives and friends, and they will put some of you to death. All men will hate you because of me. But

> not a hair of your head will perish. By standing firm you will save yourselves. (Luke 21:16-19)
>
> The day of your watchman has come,
> the day God visits you.
> ...
> Do not trust a neighbor;
> put no confidence in a friend.
> Even with her who lies in your embrace
> be careful of your words.
> For a son dishonors his father,
> a daughter rises up against her mother,
> a daughter-in-law against her mother-in-law—
> a man's enemies are members of his own household.
> But as for me, I keep watch for the Lord,
> I wait in hope for God my savior;
> my God will hear me. (Micah 7:4-7)

No, American Christians haven't been told they will be persecution free. Never-the-less, the prevailing attitude is that things will probably always be rosy. Some do expect things to get a little more intense before the pre-tribulation rapture. However, in my experience and in my evangelical circles, American Christians in general and overall expect to miss the *greatest persecution ever* by way of the pre-tribulation rapture (Matthew 24:21).

> At that time many will turn away from the faith and will betray and hate one another, and many *false prophets* will appear and deceive many people. Because of the increase of wickedness, **the love of most will grow cold**, but he who stands firm to the end will be saved. (Matthew 24:10-13, emphasis added)

[However, we can rely on this: true Christians cannot lose their salvation—Jeremiah makes it abundantly clear under the new covenant this cannot happen.

> I will make an everlasting covenant with them: I will never stop doing good to them, and I will inspire them to fear me, so that they will never turn away from me. (Jeremiah 32:40)

And Paul declared of true believers:

> He will keep you strong to the end, so that you will be blameless on the day of our Lord Jesus Christ. (1 Corinthians 1:8)]

It occurs to me that the *false prophets* in Matthew's passage are like the ones in Jeremiah's day. After these prophets foolishly prophesied that the Babylonians were not coming, the Babylonians came anyway and took them into exile and burned the Temple. The false prophets then pivoted to new prophecies that declared the articles from the Temple, the exiled king (Jehoiachin), and all the other Jewish deportees would be returned from exile within two years (Jeremiah 28:1-4). Jeremiah warned Judah to stay away from these false prophets, declaring Judah's exile would last 70 years, not two (25:11-12; 29:10).

Once the *false prophets* were proven wrong about whether the Babylonians were coming or not, they could not, even then, think that they were mistaken. They had then "received" more self-deluding prophecies. They **doubled down** on a happy message even when they were disastrously wrong with their first messaging. I imagine that they were thinking (false) happy thoughts to benefit their fellow countrymen—but they were misrepresenting God. Weigh these words carefully. Who are these future *false prophets* in Matthew 24:10-13?

[The Millerites had predicted the coming of Jesus in 1843. When this didn't occur, they tried a revised date and came up with 1844. Miller himself disavowed his prognostications after that second disappointment (called later "the Great Disappointment"), but others **doubled down** and reinterpreted the 1844 event in a spiritual way. They could not be wrong; they could not admit their method of interpretation was flawed.

Most other denominations got it right and thought the Millerites had used an incorrect system of Bible interpretation, a false "day for a year" theory among other mistakes. (Like failing to see that half of seven years was 3 ½ years; that a time, times, and a half of time was 3 ½ years; that, 1,260 days also meant 3 ½ years; that, 42 months meant 3 ½ years. There was no scriptural warrant to change 1,260 days into 1,260 years, et cetera.) These events soured many denominations on second-coming theories, so much so, they stopped studying Daniel and the end-times altogether.]

Second Thessalonians 1 & 2

Our relief from trouble and persecution is to be expected at the fiery and powerful Second Coming of Jesus—

All this is evidence that God's judgment is right, and as a result you will be counted **worthy of the kingdom of God**, for which you are suffering. God is just: He will pay back trouble to those who trouble you and give relief to you who are troubled, and to us as well. This will happen **when** the Lord Jesus is **revealed** from heaven in blazing fire with his powerful angels. He will punish those who do not know God and do not obey the gospel of our Lord Jesus...**on the day** he comes to be glorified in his holy people and to be marveled at among all those who have believed. (2 Thessalonians 1:5-10, emphasis added)

Our relief from persecution is at the **revealing** of Jesus in blazing fire with His powerful angels to "trouble" our persecutors and give relief to the "troubled" church—on **the day** that He comes to be marveled at and glorified by believers. This contrasts with the pre- and mid-tribulation views that say He first comes stealthily (and therefore **not revealed**) seven years (or 3½ years) before the Second Coming and snatches up believers in secret and in silence, leaving the world to wonder what happened.

2 Thessalonians 1:5-10 is *obviously* nothing other than Matthew 24.

The discussion of the coming of Jesus in the first chapter of 2 Thessalonians is continued in the second chapter. Without distinguishing a difference between the revelation of Jesus and His gathering of the saints in the first chapter, Paul repeats the same theme in the second chapter:

> Concerning the *coming* of our Lord Jesus Christ and our being *gathered* to him, we ask you, brothers, not to become easily unsettled or alarmed by some prophecy, report or letter supposed to have come from us, saying that the day of the Lord has already come. (2 Thessalonians 2:1-2, emphasis added)

Paul makes no distinction between the coming of Christ in the first chapter and our *gathering* to Him with His coming in the second chapter. In the first chapter, Jesus *comes* in blazing fire with His powerful angels to pay back those who persecute the church—*on the day He comes* to be glorified by His saints.

In the second chapter the theme of the coming of Jesus is equated with "the day of the Lord." Paul writes that day, however, cannot happen until the *rebellion* occurs and the man of lawlessness (the antichrist) is revealed, entering God's Temple and declaring himself to be God. The *revelation* of Christ is after the revelation of the antichrist.

The revelation of the antichrist happens in the middle of the seven-year prophecy of Daniel and also in the book of Revelation:

> It set itself up to be as great as the Prince of the host, it *took away the daily sacrifice from him*, and the place of his sanctuary was brought low. Because of *rebellion*, the host [of the saints] and the *daily sacrifice* were given over to it. It

prospered in everything it did, and truth was thrown to the ground. (Daniel 8:11-12, emphasis added)

He will confirm a covenant with many for one 'seven,' but **in the middle of that 'seven'** he will put an **end to sacrifice and offering**. And one who causes desolation will place abominations on a wing [of the temple] until the end that is decreed is poured out on him (Daniel 9:27, emphasis added).

The king will do as he pleases. He will exalt and magnify himself above every god and will say unheard-of things against the God of gods. He will be successful until the *time of wrath* is completed. (Daniel 11:36, emphasis added)

The man clothed in linen, who was above the waters, lifted his right hand and his left hand toward heaven, and I heard him swear by him who lives forever, saying, 'It will be for a **time, times and half a time** [i.e., 3 ½ years]. **When the power of the holy people** has been finally broken, all these things will be completed. (Daniel 12:7, emphasis added)

'Go and measure the temple of God and the altar... But exclude the outer court; do not measure it, because it has been given to the Gentiles. They will trample on the holy city for **42 months** [i.e., 3 ½ years]. (Revelation 11:1-2, emphasis added)

> A great and wonderous sign appeared in heaven: a woman clothed with the sun, with the moon under her feet and a crown of twelve stars on her head. (Revelation 12:1)
>
> The woman fled into the desert to a place prepared for her by God, where she might be taken care of for ***1,260 days*** [i.e., 3 ½ lunar years]. (Revelation 12:6, emphasis added)
>
> Then the dragon was enraged at the woman and went off ***to make war against the rest of her offspring***—those who obey God's commandments and ***hold to the testimony of Jesus***. (Revelation 12:17, emphasis added)
>
> The beast was given a mouth to utter proud words and blasphemies and to exercise his authority for ***forty-two months*** [i.e., 3 ½ years]. He opened his mouth to ***blaspheme God***, and to ***slander His name*** and his dwelling place and those who live in heaven. He was given power to ***make war against the saints and to conquer them***. He was given authority over every tribe, people, language and nation. (Revelation 13:5-7, emphasis added)

Some observations should be emphasized:

1. The time of the Great Tribulation is limited to 3½ years. This is stated several ways so that we would be certain of the time: at the half-way point of the seven-year covenant, a time/times/half a time, 42 months, 1260 days and 42 months (again).

2. This time period *begins* when the antichrist enters the Temple and stops "sacrifice and offerings," blaspheming the God of Heaven. The time period *finishes* when the power of God's people is finally broken.
3. This period is called *the time of wrath* (see below).
4. Satan's first attempt to destroy the people of God centers on Israel; failing that, he turns on Christians—breaking the power of the holy people, and making war on the woman's other offspring, those who hold the testimony of Jesus.
5. This scenario is world-wide: "every tribe, people, language and nation."
6. The day of the Lord, which is the coming of Christ according to Paul, cannot come until the man of lawlessness enters the Temple and declares himself to be God.
7. The day of the Lord is in turn the *not-so-secret* return of Christ in blazing fire with His powerful angels at which time Jesus gathers His people to Himself and destroys their persecutors—*after the distress of those days* (Matthew 24).

Lest we confuse the day of the Lord with the entirety of the 3½ year tribulation, read what Joel adds to the discussion. Joel 2:31 narrows the definition of the day of the Lord further by saying the sun and moon are darkened *before* the day of the Lord.

> The sun will be turned to darkness
> and the moon to blood
> *before* the coming of the great and dreadful *day of the Lord* (emphasis added)

But Jesus says in Matthew 24:29—

> Immediately *after* the distress of those days
> 'the sun will be darkened,

> and the moon will not give its light;
> the stars will fall from the sky,
> and the heavenly bodies will be shaken.' (emphasis added)

After the distress of those days the sun, moon, and stars are darkened (Matthew 24:29) but these are darkened-*before* the great and dreadful ***day of the Lord*** (Joel 2:31). In that bracketed, specific, narrow window of time, we are raptured or "gathered" to meet the Lord in the air. Paul uses the same terminology in 2 Thessalonians 2:2-3. There the day of the Lord comes sometime *after* the revelation of the antichrist—which is in the middle of the Tribulation, yet by including the teaching of Joel 2:31 and the teaching of Jesus in Matthew 24, it is *after* the distress of those days and then the ***day of the Lord*** occurs. And so, it is not a mid-tribulation rapture.

Notice that the ***Day of the Lord*** itself comes "like a thief in the night"—

> For you know very well that the day of the Lord will come ***like a thief in the night***. While people are saying, 'Peace and safety,' destruction will come on them suddenly, as labor pains on a pregnant woman, and they will not escape. (1 Thessalonians 5:2-3)

Paul says that the Thessalonians knew very well the day of the Lord is the thief-like coming Jesus talked about. How else could we understand these words?

The coming of Christ cannot happen until the antichrist sets himself up in God's Temple. The Great Tribulation (3½ years long) starts with the antichrist entering the Temple and is completed with the final breaking of the power of the holy people—the saints of Christ (Revelation 12:17 and 13:7).

Paul leaves no clue with which we could distinguish a secret coming of Jesus—not in the middle of the Tribulation nor at the beginning. We know from Matthew 24 that He comes for us *after* the distress of those days (when the sun and moon are darkened and the stars fall from the sky, Matthew 24:29)—which events are *before* the Day of the Lord. At no point in Scripture can we discern an entirely separate coming of Jesus for His saints, separated from the blazing fiery coming at the end of the Tribulation.

What kind of powerful *spell* has been cast over Bible-believers so that they cannot see this? Cannot, will not, refusing all pleading, and turning a blind eye and a deaf ear. A friend recently called the pre-tribulation rapture "an American folk religion." We add, the Pied-piper of Hamelin is playing a dark tune for the church in America and is leading it astray.

Even some who believe in the post-tribulation rapture have opted not to preach or discuss this and have adamantly and preemptively spiked a "Period!" in order to preclude all discussion. Some think that teaching what the Bible actually says about the rapture, the Tribulation, and our persecution will split the church (it may—but I pray it does not—yet we note: **the pre-tribulation rapture teaching in church history has already split the church in the past**). People may get upset (they will), but Paul taught it to the early church and to new believers anyway, even in the middle of their own persecution. In spite of this, they needed to know the whole council of God. And so do we—especially those who live near the end of days.

The first part of the *spell* that was cast over the church was to make Bible scholars see distinctions in the coming of Jesus—a pre- or mid-tribulation rapture for the church and a separate Second Coming of Jesus after the tribulation of those days.

The second part of the *spell* that was cast over those who actually take the Scriptures seriously (as opposed to those who could care less about prophecy) was to make it spread like wildfire to other churches. It then morphed into a major tenet of the faith. It became a badge of honor and is to be defended at all costs. The onslaught and momentum of this *spell* made post-tribulationists hesitate to speak at all.

However, telling the truth can hardly be a sin. The only hurt that has been caused is by those who have led the church on a wild goose chase of unsubstantiated theology.

ONE CANNOT BLAME A POST-TRIBULATIONIST FOR TRYING TO CLEAN UP THE MESS CAUSED BY OTHERS.

But notice despite the fearful teaching that we will be the target of the antichrist, Paul taught it to new believers anyway, and all the while they were already undergoing persecution!

Don't you remember that when I was with you I used to tell you these things? (2 Thessalonians 2:5)

Is It True That the Church is Not Mentioned From Chapter 4 to the End of Revelation?

It is contended by pre-tribulationists that the church is not mentioned in Revelation from chapter 4 to the end of the book—thus *implying* a pretribulation rapture before the fourth chapter of the book. Again, it should be obvious that implications are **nothing** when compared to the clear teaching of the Bible.

As we have seen, John writes that after Satan is thwarted from destroying Israel in middle of the seven-year Tribulation, he will then turn on those who hold the testimony of Jesus (Revelation 12:17). The dragon cannot reach the woman (Israel), and she goes into the desert for the last 3½ years of the Tribulation.

> Then the dragon was enraged at the woman and went off to make war against the rest of her offspring—those who obey God's commands and *hold the testimony of Jesus*. (Revelation 12:17, emphasis added)

Some say these believers *who hold the testimony of Jesus* are Tribulation saints—those who do believe but only after the pre- or mid-tribulation rapture of the church. Then one can reasonably point out that the word or idea of "the church" (the Bride of Christ) is not mentioned or indicated from Revelation 4 to the end of the book.

But it is not genius if one first **assumes** that the pre- or mid-tribulation rapture is true, and then concludes the church is not one and the same with those who **hold the testimony of Jesus**. And then because of this assumption, it is deduced that the church is not mentioned from Revelation 4 through the end of the book! The **assumption**, however, cannot be made, because it flies in the face of all we have discovered so far—passages that state specifically that the church is gathered at the end of the Tribulation, a post-tribulation rapture of the church.

It would be more natural, in light of the passages that declare unequivocally our gathering is at the Second Coming, to conclude that John's message in Revelation 12:17 was a warning to the church. This passage matches what Jesus said would be the worst persecution ever. So, we conclude those who **hold the testimony of Jesus** must be the church.

In addition, that this is the worst persecution ever is probably related to its scope—it is world-wide; it will happen in **all** nations (Matthew 24:9). It is also true that Satan has been unleashed on the whole world without restraint. That is why it would be unprecedented—and, after the return of Christ, it will never be repeated again.

This is scary—for sure. But scaring the saints into believing or preferring a pre-tribulation rapture is not good Bible exegesis—it is eisegesis, which includes reading into the text one's own biases. Scare tactics do not make pre-or mid- tribulation theology true—it just makes it more convenient and makes many more saints comfortable in believing that the rapture of the church is before the Tribulation. This, unfortunately, sets them up for complete failure.

When and Then

We already noticed the use of time language in 2 Thessalonians 1:6,7—our persecutors get their just deserts and we get relief from persecution **when** Jesus comes back in blazing fire with His powerful angels.

1 Corinthians also uses the time formula **when** and **then**. Paul writes, "The dead will be raised imperishable, and we will be *changed*," thus once again using the order of resurrection that was already established by Jesus in John 11.

Paul continues—

> For the perishable must clothe itself with the imperishable, and the mortal with immortality. **When** the perishable has been clothed with the imperishable, and the mortal with immortality, **then** the saying that is written will come true: 'Death has been swallowed up in victory.' (1 Corinthians 15:54, emphasis added)

We are to get our new bodies, we will be *changed* as Paul wrote, when death is swallowed up in victory. So, all we need to establish is **when** death will be swallowed up in victory in order to nail down the timing of the rapture—the time when we get changed in a twinkling into our new clothing. Since Paul cites Old Testament Scripture to show the timing of this, all we need to do is find the text and the context.

Paul is quoting from Isaiah—

> On this mountain the LORD Almighty will prepare a feast of rich food for all people, a banquet of aged wine—the best meats and the finest of wines. On this mountain he will destroy the **shroud** that enfolds all peoples, the sheet that covers all nations; **he will swallow up death forever.** (Isaiah 25:6-8, emphasis added)

The context preceding Isaiah 25:8 explains Paul's timing for receiving our new clothes. The prior passage setting up this marvelous re-clothing is Isaiah 24 which sets the stage for death being swallowed up in victory. Within this context, we discover *death is (definitely) swallowed up* at the end of the Tribulation, at the return of the King, and after the earth is destroyed.

> See, the LORD is going to lay waste the earth and devastate it...The earth will be completely laid waste and totally plundered...The earth dries up and withers...The earth is defiled by its people; they have disobeyed the laws, violated the statutes and **broken the everlasting covenant** [i.e., the Good News of Jesus and His Kingdom]... Therefore a curse consumes the earth; its people must bear their guilt. Therefore earth's inhabitants are burned up, and very few are left...The earth is broken up, and the earth is split asunder, ...so heavy upon it is the guilt of its rebellion that it falls—**never to rise again**...The **moon** will be abashed, the **sun** ashamed; **for the LORD Almighty will reign** on Mount Zion and in Jerusalem and before its elders, gloriously. (Isaiah 24, various verses, emphasis added)

Isaiah continues in the next chapter:

> The Sovereign LORD will wipe away the tears from all faces; he will remove the disgrace of **his people** from all the earth. (Isaiah 25:8, emphasis added)

Isaiah 26:19 adds:

> But your dead will live; their bodies will rise. You who dwell in the dust, wake up and shout for joy. Your dew is like the dew of the morning; the earth will give birth to her dead.

The phrase *"Death is swallowed up in victory"* is at the end of the world, and at the end of the Tribulation when *the moon will be abashed, the sun ashamed*, and at the beginning of the Kingdom of God on earth. **When** this happens, **then** this happens. **When** the earth meets its doom and at the coming of the King, **then** death is swallowed up in victory for **Christ's own—His people**. When Jesus comes back after the world is devastated, we get our new bodies.

This is most certainly a post-tribulation event in context if you read it unbiasedly. Isaiah **does not write** *"he will swallow up death forever"* **before** his description of the destruction of the earth; he does not write it at the beginning of chapter 24.

If Isaiah had written *"he will swallow up death forever"* **first** and then followed it with the description of the destruction of the earth, **then** and only then could we definitively say that Paul meant a pre-tribulation rapture. In fact, were this true, pre-tribulation theologians would be all over it. The *reverse*, however, is true—**first** the destruction of the earth, **then** we get our new bodies. This fits the pattern of Paul discovering the order of resurrection from what Jesus said to Martha.

The Argument That We Are Exempt from Wrath

Recently I began an intense back-and-forth with another "Martha" whom I had met in Jerusalem. She is very sincere in her beliefs, and I could by no means convince her that the post-tribulation rapture was the correct view to take. But I do wonder why.

I contended that the pre-tribulation argument had *zero* plainly understood verses—not inferences but actual verses, to back up the claim that the church will be raptured before the Tribulation. Rather than producing unequivocal biblical references to a pre-tribulation rapture that would correct the arguments presented above, for her part, the argument was an inference that the pre-tribulation rapture was correct, because Christians are not destined for **wrath**.

> God did not appoint us to suffer **wrath** but to receive **salvation** through our Lord Jesus Christ... Therefore encourage one another and build each other up, just as in fact you are doing. (1 Thessalonians 5:9,11, emphasis added)

Many fervently believe God promises that the church will miss the wrath of the seven-year Tribulation. **Wrath** to them is the Tribulation, and indeed it is called **the time of wrath** in Daniel 11:36. However, in Daniel's narrative, it is started and completed in 3½ years, not seven.

To some interpreters, "salvation" only means a pre-tribulation rapture. By itself, taken in isolation, this could be a reasonable argument. Taken with the whole of Scripture, it is not. Certainly, enduring a time of **wrath** is an uncomfortable thought.

Many hold forth that a post-tribulation rapture is not comforting, nor is it encouraging. But one could also argue that Jeremiah's message was not comforting nor was it encouraging: "Surrender to the Babylonians or die!" Also, Jesus' message to His disciples—we are not above our Master. If He was on the receiving end of persecution, then His disciples should expect that, too (Matthew 10:24-25). His message is also not comforting, nor could it be conceived of as encouraging in the sense that pre-tribulationists mean comforting and encouraging.

Pre-tribulationists interpret **wrath** to mean "the Tribulation" and "salvation" to mean "rapture." At first blush, the word **wrath** might be defined as 3½ years of Tribulation as Daniel indicates. At least the second half of Daniel's 70th seven might be meant—the Great Tribulation—but not a seven-year Tribulation.

But notice in the whole context of the argument, there are no verses in the New Testament that promise an imminent return of Christ. There are no verses that say a pre-tribulation rapture or a mid-tribulation rapture is what we should expect. Saying that **wrath** means the seven-year Tribulation and therefore we would not be here for it is **at best** an inference—and it is the emotionally preferred outcome to their argument. The inference of a mid-tribulation rapture is only a shade better.

To **infer** from Paul's use of the word **wrath** that the seven-year Tribulation is meant (or the 3½ year Great Tribulation) is a weak inference that only gets stronger in our imagination when we emphasize the gravity of the Tribulation and its scary events. No, it won't be pleasant, but the old adage "A coward dies a thousand times, a brave man only once" is an important thing to remember.

An appeal to 2 Peter 2:9 could show that the pre- or mid-tribulation rapture is a possibility:

> The Lord knows how to rescue godly men from *trials* and to hold the unrighteous for the day of judgment... (Emphasis added)

But if **elect** were defined as Tribulation saints (or defined as the Jewish nation) in Matthew 24 instead of the church itself, and *trials* defined as the Tribulation, then God would also be *obligated* to see these **elect** through the *trials* that come on the earth during the time of the Tribulation. If, theoretically, He can do it for Tribulation saints or the Jewish nation during the Tribulation, then He should be able to do it for the church (**the elect**) in the Tribulation too. And the **elect** of Matthew 24 as we have already seen can only mean the bride of Christ, His church.

The language of a thief-like coming is presented to us in a post-tribulation context (Revelation 16*). Our rescue from persecution coincides with the day Jesus returns at His revelation in fire and power to destroy those who "trouble" the church and resist the King and His kingdom. He destroys those who persecute His followers, and who disregard the message of salvation (2 Thessalonians 1).

[*A famous speaker (who also believes in a pre-tribulation rapture) came to our church in February and actually read aloud Revelation 16; he ignored its direct message and weakly (or not at all) tried to explain away the significance of the thief-like coming of Jesus in the middle of the battle of Armageddon.]

So, what wrath are we promised to miss? **Wrath** could be juxtaposed in 1 Thessalonians 5:9 with the idea of **salvation** from God's wrath for our sins—not a pre- or mid-tribulation rapture. This hope of a pre- or mid-tribulation rapture is taught nowhere—it is a theory that has no biblical support. If it is taught somewhere else—produce the verses! Job 6:24 says:

> Teach me and I will be quiet;
> Show me where I have been wrong.
> How painful are honest words!
> But what do your arguments prove?

In any case—one could also say with great legitimacy that **wrath** comes in Revelation at the very end of the Tribulation with "the great day of their **wrath** has come, and who can stand?" (Revelation 6:17, emphasis added). Could *this* be the **wrath** Paul meant we would miss; the **wrath** displayed at "the great and dreadful day of the LORD"?

It is tortured logic to assume that if we choose the implied option we prefer, the rest of Scripture can be ignored. The argument fails when we attempt to account for contrary verses. Our choice of the seven-year Tribulation **wrath** is derailed when we attempt a *comprehensive* argument for a pre- or mid-tribulation rapture theology. We must be able to account for clear statements that we will be rescued from persecution on the ***same day*** that Jesus descends from heaven in flaming fire with His mighty angels.

And also, innocent believers *do* sometimes go through the same punishment given to unbelievers.

This is what the LORD says:

> 'If those who do not deserve to drink the cup must drink it [i.e., the good guys], why should you [i.e., the bad guys] go unpunished? You will not go unpunished, but must drink it. (Jeremiah 49:12)

This means the guilty together with the innocent suffered hardship, starvation, and death at the hands of the Babylonians. Maybe the attitude of the innocent makes all the difference. For one it is punishment; for the other it is the patient endurance of the saints. [See the astonishing perseverance of Armenian

Christians who have suffered for being Christians, century after century (*Judgment unto Truth*, Ephraim k. Jernazian).]

To lay it out, we have **wrath** defined different ways:

1. In 1 Thessalonians 5:9 **wrath** means the seven-year Tribulation. Therefore, we are exempt from it.
2. In 1 Thessalonians 5:9 **wrath** means the 3½ year Great Tribulation. In Daniel 11:36, **wrath** is juxtaposed with the time of the antichrist (so, in this case 3½ years, not 7 years). Therefore, coupled with 1 Thessalonians 5:9, we are exempt from it.
3. **Wrath** means the wrath of God against sin and the punishment of hell (Romans 5:9). Therefore, with 1 Thessalonians 5:9, we are exempt from this punishment through our faith in Christ.
4. **Wrath** is at the great and awesome day of the Lord at the end of the Tribulation (Revelation 6:17). Therefore, with 1 Thessalonians 5:9, believers are exempt from it.

All by themselves in isolation, to some interpreters, numbers [1] and [2] may be conclusive. Mid-tribulationists say we will not be here for the time of **wrath** that is coming on the earth and that it is not a seven-year period, but rather 3½ years.

However, post-tribulationists urge caution. We could be shielded from the **wrath** that God brings on the earth without being removed from the earth by rapture. Lot was rescued from Sodom by being dragged out of the city before it was destroyed. Noah was saved from the flood without leaving the earth.

Not only that, if we decide that number [2] is conclusive and Christians are raptured in the middle of the Tribulation, the other Scriptures that definitively say that we are rescued *after* the Tribulation of those days must be accounted for.

Paul's clear verses that describe our gathering to Christ in the same terms that Jesus used in Matthew 24 (1 Thessalonians

4:15), militates against the definitions of **wrath** in [1] and [2]. That we get our new bodies after the Tribulation is clear from Isaiah 24 and 25—this also militates against the definitions of **wrath** in [1] and [2]. Our persecution ends on the same day that Jesus returns in blazing fire with His powerful angels—this, again, militates against the ideas of [1] and [2]. The thief-like coming is repeated by Jesus in Revelation 16, clearly indicating the church is rescued at the end, militating against [1] and [2]. The Day of the Lord comes **like a thief in the night**, at the dimming of the sun, moon, and stars, after the Tribulation of those days. This militates against adopting [1] or [2].

All of these passages tell us that only number [3] or [4] could be what Paul meant by **wrath** in 1 Thessalonians 5:9.

The Time of Trial

Pre-tribulation theologians see a promise to miss the very *time* of the Tribulation in Revelation 3:10—

> Since you have kept my command to endure patiently, I will also keep you from the **hour*** of trial that is going to come upon the whole world to test those who live on the earth. (Revelation 3:10, emphasis added)

First of all, a guarantee to be saved from the "*time* of Jacob's trouble" is also promised to Israel:

> How awful that day will be! None will be like it. It will be a *time of trouble* for Jacob, but **he will be saved out of it**. 'In that day,' declares the Lord Almighty, ... no longer will foreigners enslave them. Instead, they will serve the Lord their God and David their king [i.e., the Messiah]. (Jeremiah 30:7-9, emphasis added)

By this, the implication that the pre-tribulation rapture must be true, because we never even enter into the *time* of the Tribulation is not shown to be a mandatory interpretation. A mid-tribulation rapture cannot be assumed from what we see promised to Israel for the identical time period. Being saved out of the time of Tribulation does not *of necessity* mean removal from earth to heaven with a secret rapture.

Besides that, the time of "the *hour* of trial" is further defined for us in Revelation 14:7, "... the *hour**of his judgment has come" and in 14:15, "The *hour** to reap has come" (the gathering of the saints). This passage depicts one like 'a son of man' seated on a white cloud using a sickle to reap the harvest of believers, as Matthew 24:30 has already described. There the Son of Man comes on the clouds of the sky to gather His *elect*. This is *after* the distress of the Tribulation (Matthew 24:29).

Since the Greek word for *hour** is the same for all three passages: 3:10, 14:7, and 14:15, it would be natural to see these as one and the same or related events in the book of Revelation. Following the harvest that the Son of Man reaps in Revelation 14:15, grapes are then gathered to judgment, throwing them into the great winepress of God's *wrath* (14:17-19). This matches the order of Matthew 24—first the *elect* are gathered and then the gathering of *two men in a field* and *two women grinding with a hand mill* "one taken [i.e., to judgment] and the other left."

These verses tell us that the "*hour* of trial" in 3:10 is at the end of the Tribulation. *The **hour of trial*** we are promised to miss is not seven years long, nor is it 3½ years long. This indicates the *wrath* we are exempt from—the great winepress of God's *wrath* at the end of the tribulation.

A Poignant Conclusion

Long ago, Israel faced a fork in the road. Over and over again, Jeremiah had been prophesying gloom and destruction for Jerusalem. King Zedekiah waffled back and forth between listening to Jeremiah and throwing him into the muddy cistern. The prophet was accused of *treason* for telling the besieged population of Jerusalem to surrender to the Babylonians, because he had advised them that this was their only life-saving option.

It became violent one day early in the reign of Jehoiakim when Jeremiah spoke to the people and said that unless they turned from their evil ways the house of God would become as desolate as Shiloh (the former house of God), and the city would become an object of cursing. He was seized by the priests, the prophets and the people, who said to him, "You must die" (Jeremiah 26:8).

However, some of the elders and officials along with some of the people intervened. They remembered the prophet Micah of Moresheth who had ministered in the days of good king Hezekiah. He had prophesied that the Temple would be overgrown with thickets, and Zion would be plowed like a field (Micah 3:12). They observed that no one had put him to death for these prophecies. A little later Jeremiah declared:

> But the prophet who prophesies peace will be recognized as one truly sent by the Lord only if his prediction comes true. (Jeremiah 28:9)

Therefore, I respectfully ask, "When have the words of Jesus been abrogated about the persecution of the church down through the ages?"

There has never been teaching in the Bible for a pre- or mid-tribulation rapture, but there are several clear and plain verses that indicate the coming of Jesus for His own is a post-tribulation event.

> 1. At best, those who hold tenaciously to the pre-tribulation rapture have a promise that believers are not under the **wrath** of God and therefore, they conclude, they will miss the Tribulation. But we have also seen that the Great Day of His **wrath** is pinpointed at the end of the Tribulation. And their tenaciously held inference of a pre- or mid-tribulation rapture flies in the face of clear Scripture to the contrary.
>
> In many cases, those who love the word of God and are part of the "Bible-believing" church have fallen for a feel-good promise that is taught nowhere in the Bible (I call this fall a ***spell***). It is comfortable; it is a comforting message; it is easy to believe—but only if debate is cut off and the opposing view is ridiculed. Scripture for the pre- or mid-tribulation rapture do not exist.
>
> If you still don't believe this, get the best books that defend the pre- and mid-tribulation rapture and look up every verse cited. Write down the ones that are *conclusive*, that cannot be challenged with plainer, less complicated interpretations, and that are **not inferences**.
>
> They must simultaneously account for all the Scriptures. If these cannot account for the post-tribulation verses that we have discussed, then the pre- or mid-tribulation

theories are a hoax. To make a coherent argument, the verses of Scripture that we have reviewed *must* be accounted for.

Prepare yourself for the house of cards to fall. Examine your commitment to Christ. Is it based on "My God would never do that to me!" or, "I cannot suffer for believing in Christ."? Or is it based on believing in the risen Savior who died for our sins and promises us a place at His table in the kingdom to come?

2. I also *want* the pre- or mid-tribulation raptures to be true—that is my personal preference even now. I argued for the pre-tribulation rapture long ago in Bible college. I looked up every verse in *Things to Come* to be able to defend what I had been taught. To my chagrin, I found absolutely no verses that taught the pre-tribulation rapture. Not even one.

I sought out every professor that I thought could help me graduate Bible college by showing me where I was wrong, but they came up short. I loved these professors and wanted them to be right, and conversely, for me to be wrong—but their answers were surprisingly weak.

Initially, I was denied my diploma on graduation day with my fellow seniors. I was refused graduation at that time.

3. We conclude that the church has been fed a false hope.

The Devastation False Promises Cause—The Sudden Distress of the Church in the Tribulation

God Himself has supposedly promised that the church cannot and *will not* undergo the Tribulation. Those who believe in the pre- or mid-tribulation rapture think that they have been promised that the church won't even enter into the *time* of the Tribulation. Their loving Father will always be there for them—but then, suddenly, He won't seem to be. Out of the blue, the church will find itself in the midst of the Tribulation or even in the Great Tribulation.

Feelings of betrayal and bitterness will come raging in. Faith in a good God will wane and tremble in a cutting wind of hopelessness. A sense of complete bewilderment will overcome the American part of the family of God. Death of faith will and must stalk each one. They will have been mentally and spiritually unprepared and will not have been warned.

It has happened before. At the end of the 19th century and the beginning of the 20th century, Armenian Christians were slaughtered in large numbers. Multiple events were orchestrated by the Turkish government and perpetrated by many policemen, soldiers, and ordinary citizens of the Islamic regime. Approximately 1,200,000 died miserable deaths. It is one of the best attested holocausts in history. [The term holocaust was first used of the Armenian slaughter.]

At the outset of this, Armenian men were rounded up for work details after they were disarmed. They were marched off and slaughtered out of earshot and out of sight. Tricked into thinking they were going to resettle with their husbands to the east, the women were forced to trek across Anatolia with little forewarning. Women and children were **mercilessly** marched hundreds of miles to their gruesome deaths along the way. In fact, the perpetrators thought the Armenians deserved their fate.

On this ill-fated march, one bewildered soul asked an Armenian prelate why they weren't warned by their Christian leaders. But there could be no response to this; what possible comfort could he have given in the middle of their despair and after the monumental failure of their clergy?

Valleys in Turkey were filled with the dead. Harems were filled with unwilling Christian girls and Christian women. Mothers cut off their noses and their daughters' noses to make them too ugly to violate. [HEAR ME!] As the forced march concluded its journey across Turkey, these unfortunate Christians left their bones to bleach in the Iraqi desert sun as silent witnesses to this forgotten holocaust. All this happened only one hundred years ago.

To this day Turkey denies that anything happened. But, twenty thousand dispatches by American diplomats alone, decrying and documenting this mass slaughter, were sent to Washington. Today, we are hardly aware of this atrocity, but our great-great grandfathers and grandmothers sent over $100,000,000 to try to help Armenian Christians. This would be one billion dollars in today's money. [See *Armenian Golgotha*, Grigoris Balakian and *The Burning Tigris, The Armenian Genocide and America's Response*, Peter Balakian].

Use your imagination to grasp the scope of this. Beliefs have consequences. Bad, non-biblical beliefs have worse consequences. Use your imagination. In retrospect, it seems we serve a different God than Christians have served for the last twenty centuries. Isn't that so?

Missionaries in Muslim lands who introduced the happy songs of American Christianity were frustrated with the response of their congregations. They couldn't sing them—they were incongruous with their experience. Once the missionaries understood the long-term persecution of Christians in these lands, they began to understand the solemn and sad songs these Christians sing.

Consider the centuries of annihilation of Christians by Islam. The churches in the Middle East before Islam's conquest were uncountable—but we have forgotten this fact. Horrors beyond belief on a monstrous scale awaited this faithful church. Defections from Christ to Islam were common. These defectors had been members of the Christian community, but when the time came to lay down their lives for the Savior, they defected and even helped the oppressors oppress their former co-religionists.

The total scope of the rape, plunder, and enslaving of hapless victims in the West and in the Middle East by Islam is almost totally forgotten by Christians in the wake of self-flagellation over the *comparatively* minor atrocities committed by the Crusaders. The nine crusades spanned 200 years and were on and off again. The terror of Islam has been fourteen centuries long almost without interruption somewhere in the world. Why are we afraid to remember this? [See: *The Decline of Eastern Christianity Under Islam*, Bat Ye'or.]

The recent 19th and 20th centuries were incredibly bad for Christians worldwide. [See: *By Their Blood, Christian Martyrs of the 20th Century*, James and Marti Hefley.]

Worthy of the Kingdom of God

It is no good to say that God would not leave His children behind to suffer in the Tribulation, because in all of church history it *has* happened. But Jesus warned His people that this would be the case—and that, in and of itself, is comforting. He knew and He warned and He shared in their sufferings. In all these centuries, for the most part, the Christian church was found ***worthy of the kingdom of God*** (2 Thessalonians 1:5).

Jesus once speculated,

> When the Son of Man comes, will he find faith on the earth? (Luke 18:8)

And He declared—

> Then you will be handed over to be persecuted and put to death, and you will be hated by ***all*** nations because of me. At that time many ***will turn away from the faith*** and will betray and hate each other, and many ***false prophets*** will appear and deceive many people. Because of the increase of wickedness, ***the love of most will grow cold***, but he who stands firm to the end will be saved. (Matthew 24:9-13, emphasis added)

I used to think that these ***false prophets*** were outside the church. Now I believe they could be inside the church during the Tribulation, still trying to convince the church that it would soon leave the earth. They will **double down** and give false encouragement like the false prophets in Jeremiah's day. Ignore them.

I am pleading with you! We dare not promise something contrary to what our Lord promised would be the lot of His followers in every age and, at the end, in *all* nations.

In my experience, those who believe in a post-tribulation rapture have been forced into silence. They have been scorned and laughed at. They have been steam-rolled and left behind in the rush to loudly proclaim the pre-tribulation rapture. Doctrinal statements preclude their participation in the leadership of the church—they certainly cannot teach what they know. They have sometimes been told to find another church.

A few have learned this lesson well and refuse to proclaim the whole counsel of God in the face of opposition, indifference, and condescension. They have sometimes lost their jobs or have been denied positions in their churches. All this in the face of relentless teaching and preaching of something not found in the Scriptures.

This same unbelief and ridicule met those few Jews in pre-WWII Europe who knew persecution was coming and who loudly proclaimed that the Jews needed to get out. Unfortunately, by the 1930s, Jews were completely assimilated into German culture—why should they listen to this? It was hard to believe that decorated Jewish veterans who had fought for their Fatherland in World War I could be treated as pariahs a few years later. Ask yourself: Is the western church fully assimilated into its culture?

Outside of Germany, but in the same vein, the now famous Elie Wiesel had sympathized with one of these watchmen. Moishe had been deported from Hungary to Poland along with other Jewish foreigners. Crossing the border, unloaded from trucks, and deposited in a forest, they were shot into a trench they had been forced to dig. Moishe, who was shot in the leg, played dead and was able to escape back to Hungary to warn the Jewish village of Sighet that the Nazis wanted them all dead.

But they could not and would not believe him. They told each other, "Hitler could not destroy an entire people!" They suspected that Moishe was mad. They refused to believe him and refused to listen. They assured themselves that the Germans were over the border and not in Hungary. When the German army invaded Hungary, they **doubled down** and assured themselves that the capital was a long way away.

Moishe kept shouting in the synagogue, "Just listen to me!" He was ignored until it was too late. Elie, though he didn't believe Moishe either, tried to understand the man as he moaned, All I wanted them to do was just listen to me! (*Night*, by Elie Wiesel).

Some Armenians in the early part of the 20th century knew enough to discern the handwriting on the wall. They knew from previous atrocities perpetrated against their fellow religionists that the trouble would not stop. They urged a defensive stance against a slow-rolling (sometimes swift) slaughter across the land.

Many Armenians refused to believe and continued to cooperate with Turkish authorities even after miserable caravans of abused, naked, raped, and starving Armenian refugees rolled through their towns. Many **doubled down** on being good citizens and accepted anything that the Turks demanded until it was too late (*Judgment unto Truth*, Ephraim K. Jernazian).

The Holocaust (the Shoah) was beyond human understanding. It *is* beyond human understanding. Many books have been written about the reasons for the Shoah, but in my opinion, they all fall short in explaining it (for example, *Why? Explaining the Holocaust*, Peter Hayes). Peter Hayes brilliantly explains what he can, but the key ingredient is always missing from these books that attempt to explain the Holocaust. They must fall short, because they do not understand the underlying, seemingly irrational impetus for this indescribable event.

I don't want to be simplistic, but most leave out the religious and spiritual dimension. Otherwise, it is outside of human reasoning to imagine how Nazi Germany happened. Why was the Shoah carried out in historically "Christian" Europe (mainly) against millions of helpless Jews? What kind of Christianity was it—was it only cultural Christianity? How could antisemitism spread in a continent whose Scriptures proclaim that the Jews are beloved for the sake of the Patriarchs?

How much did 19th century universities in Germany and their Higher Criticism undermine the Bible and the Christian faith? What was the religion of the Nazis? How deeply were the Germans into spiritism and folk religion and pagan rituals? How much influence did authentic Christianity exert in politics? What demonic force led Hitler and his minions to the conclusion that Jews were to blame for all the woes of post-World War I?

Why did "Christianized" Germans collude and conclude with the Turks before both world wars that Armenian Christians deserved to die? (Diabolically, German soldiers stationed in Turkey called Christian Armenians "Armenian Jews.") The earlier Holocaust against Armenian Christians became the how-to template to destroy the Jews twenty years later. But the real *"why?"* is not solved by simply looking into the motives of the perpetrators and the circumstances of either Holocaust. The real question might be asked, Who was the puppet master behind Muslim Arabs and Turks, the Germans and many Europeans?

Why did many Jews favor atheistic Communism over Judeo-Christian values even though its founder, Karl Marx, was a supremely vile man? Why do Orthodox Jews every ten years or so blame the secularism of German Jews for the Holocaust? Why was there a statue of Budha at the festival in Israel before the 7th of October? Why is Israel a very secular state? Do we really believe Paul that a curse lies on those who do not love the Lord—1 Corinthians 16:22? (See John 3:18.)

In the spiritual realm, Satan's *rational* thought was and *is* to destroy Israel. God is his enemy, and thus for Satan, it is *rational* to destroy God's people. [Ultimately, it is irrational since he cannot hope to defeat God.] Islamic theology claims that the Muslim vision for the end-times cannot occur until every Jew in the world is killed. This is satanic, yet it is irrational and inexplicable from a mere human point of view—unless we take notice of the puppet master.

Politics and historical realities aside, it is unexplainable that any group of people raised in the Judeo-Christian milieu could perpetrate (and tolerate) what happened to the Jewish people during World War II. A gigantic, ancient spell must have overcome the continent of Europe.

Those who write about the Shoah should have informed themselves about Israel's satanic adversary. But they don't seem to have done that. In the same vein, the American church in general must not have informed itself about the sad history of the persecution of the church down through the centuries. Otherwise, they would not have fallen for the propaganda that tells them they will not undergo the Tribulation.

Before World War II, another prescient man, Ze'ev Vladimir Jabotinski, the founder of Zionist nationalism, was pursued twice by ultra-Orthodox assassins, trying to silence him for advocating immediate mass Jewish emigration from Europe (*Israel's Bible Bloc*, Dennis "Avi" Lipkin). [The irrational thought to kill someone who threatened the *status quo* trumped the commandment not to murder.] The Orthodox hierarchy had firmly established their way of life in "civilized" Eastern Europe. They underestimated Satan's rational/irrational hate. The prescient watchman lived; large numbers of those he tried to warn died.

Seeing Satan's rage that has already played out against the Jews and the Christians, in the future, what are Satan's *rational/ irrational* goals against the people of Israel and the people who belong to Christ?

The Watchman's Duty

This is a sad duty for me. Yet, I feel compelled after all these years to stand up with this manifesto to try to increase the discussion and to warn of a disastrous theology that permeates the church in America. I believe churches who are prepared with the truth of what will happen in the future will survive the contest better than those who have been given a false narrative. "Surviving" in this context is staying true to Christ to the end.

Just show me how I have misunderstood the Bible's message, and show me coherent verses, not unsupported inferences that say the pre- or mid-tribulation raptures are true, and I will join you. Otherwise, I have blown the trumpet and fulfilled my duty as a *watchman* (Ezekiel 33:2-5).

Other than this manifesto, I don't know how to break through the tradition, the fog, the *spell* that envelops my fellow Christians. Perhaps blowing the trumpet louder will make a difference. What would be the result if I were to shout out in your church service "Just listen to me!"?

Two Commands to the Church

There are two specific commands to the church in 1 John. The two commands are to believe in Jesus and to love our brothers in Christ (1 John 3:23).

If the pre-tribulation rapture is so very true and so certain and plain, why the nasty treatment of brothers and sisters who hold to a post-tribulation view? Why do doctrinal statements include the imminent return of Christ and a pre-tribulation rapture that automatically preclude leadership roles in the life of the church for dissenting views?

Could it be that *fear* trumps treating brothers and sisters in Christ as brothers and sisters in Christ? Or is it because the argument for the pre-tribulation rapture is far from strong? Maybe it needs an extra boost by being included with major tenets of the faith?

The pre- or mid-tribulation raptures are indeed weak arguments: one professor at a seminary was counting the number of times a Greek preposition was used the way he wanted it to be used in order to prove the pre-tribulation rapture—as if that would make a difference in any kind of argument!

I have been shouted at by a leader of my denomination, screamed at by a distraught church member, initially denied graduation from Bible college, denied entry into my Bible college's seminary, denied numerous church jobs—even a job on the mission field—and kicked out of teaching Sunday School at my home church. An in-person interview for a pastorate I was applying for was abruptly and rudely ended when they heard I believed in a post-tribulation rapture*. Even a fellow Bible college graduate ended all discussion with a resounding, in-your-face, "Period!"

*Lest you think I was using subterfuge in applying to this church, I was not. My father, who had hosted my family in his home for a year waiting for me to find a pastorate, grew impatient and asked me to leave out my views of the rapture before this interview. He thought my winning personality would overcome all opposition once they got to know me.

Dad had no idea the depth of the "Bible-believing" church's aversion to the post-tribulation view! I acquiesced to him with heavy heart. At the end of the interview with the pulpit committee, when I revealed my stand on the Tribulation and the Rapture, their interim pastor leaped to his feet and shook hands all round with the committee, signaling he wanted nothing more to do with this. The interview was over. He did not shake my hand.

Can you think of a reason why fellow believers in Christ should be treated this way? Can you think of a reason why Bible believers *do* treat believers in a post-tribulation rapture this way? Better yet, can you think of a Bible verse that teaches a pre- or mid-tribulation rapture?

Pastors know the consequences for stepping out of line. This mirrors some of my fellow seniors at Bible college years ago—they just plowed ahead and signed the doctrinal statement that espoused imminency anyway. They would think about other views of the rapture after graduation. I suppose they feared their fellow-believers would throw them out into the cold, too. Do churches not grow if they talk about suffering for their faith?

Snappy come-backs like, "I don't even eat *Post Toasties*!" are unwelcome in deadly serious discussions. Why can't the church have serious discussions on this topic?

So, I have little hope that the *spell* will lift any time soon. Maybe in a decade or two, when the time of Christ's coming draws near, someone will find this manifesto and heed the warning.

An Afterword: Here Are Some Things We Can Do

[1] Encourage thoughtful Bible study on this topic. Look up every verse mentioned in your study books to see what things are *really* so or what things are just inferences, or circular reasoning, or just-so (unverifiable) arguments, or confirmation bias. Weed out unintentional inferences (posing as real arguments) from solid verses and then make your stand. Study the doctrine of suffering and the sad history of the church under persecution.

[2] Warn fellow believers if you see a problem with the pre-tribulation rapture. Don't fail to say something and don't equivocate. Become a watchman—sound the alarm. Be advised, however—no one will like you or appreciate you for being a watchman.

[3] Your actions in all this must conform to Jesus' command to love the brothers. Though loving the brothers is a neglected teaching, we must do all we can with the gentleness and kindness and directness of Jesus as we fulfill our duties as watchmen. Sometimes love compels a direct wakeup call—to love means to warn.

And even if you still believe in a pre-tribulation rapture, fearlessly advocate on behalf of those who are of a different persuasion—after all, we are fellow believers in Christ, and this issue does not rise to the same level of doctrine as the deity of Christ—*by far*. Promote open discussion.

[4] Read Luke 22.

[5] Act like you are a pilgrim, just passing through this life to a better world. Don't cling to this life as if this were all there is. "A coward dies a thousand times, a brave man only once."

[6] Make sure that you are a believer—even if you think you have been one for years and years—examine yourself to see if you are in the faith (2 Corinthians 13:5). See to it no bitter root grows in the church to cause trouble that will defile many (Hebrews 12:15).

[7] Have a proactive stance that helps believers around the world who are being persecuted right now (Hebrews 13:3).

[8] When "you see all these things," run for the hills. Make sure you have a well-thought-out plan about what to do next or what to do if.

[9] Accept that you may have to die for your faith in Christ like countless believers before you. Therefore, practice dying daily. Prepare your heart to stay true no matter what happens. Those who stand firm to the end will be saved (Matthew 24:13). And this even if you have to do it alone, even if you have to die alone.

[10] Settle in your mind that you may have to go into captivity (Revelation 13:10).

[11] Pray that you may be able to escape all these things and to stand before the Son of Man (Luke 21:36).

[12] Remember: The Great Tribulation lasts only 1,260 days—then Jesus returns.

What All Three Views of the Rapture Can Do Together

[13] The last one is the most complex and takes the most faith and the most study.

I published *The Temple and the Lost Tribes of Israel* in 2022 that describes two prophecies that "hasten the day of Christ." It concerns two things that Jewish theologians are waiting for: (1) the restoration of the ten lost tribes of Israel and (2) rebuilding the Temple in Jerusalem (see Zechariah 6:15). [One of the requirements Jewish theologians have stated for the rebuilding of the Temple is for the Gentile world to ask them to do it!] These two I maintain will speed the coming of the day of Christ (2 Peter 3:12). We also do it for the sake of evangelism: "And so all Israel will be saved" (Romans 11:26).

Advancing these two helps to hasten the day of Christ. Yet, for those who believe in a pre- or mid-tribulation rapture, you might expect that those who believe in a post-tribulation rapture would *not* want to hasten the day.

Yet, consider what it sounds like to an Orthodox Jew to hear tourists of the pre-tribulation rapture persuasion encourage Israel to rebuild the Temple. A Jewish author has written about his scorn for Christians who want the Jews to rebuild the Temple so true believers can be raptured—only to leave behind unbelieving Jews to their well-deserved fate—what Orthodox Jews refer to as "Jacob's Trouble" (Jeremiah 30:7). We call this the Great Tribulation. This sounded to him not only self-serving but also cruel.

This perception is real (deserved or not). It is recounted in *The End of Days: Fundamentalism and the Struggle for the Temple Mount*, by Gershom Gorenberg. His book drips with acerbic comments and scorn for these Christians (he references Hal Lindsey, et cetera.). The Temple Institute in old Jerusalem carried Gorenberg's book as a warning to Christians who had uncaringly espoused such views.

I wrote to the International Director at the Temple Institute to express my sorrow at this. I told him what the New Testament really says—that Jews would be rescued out of the time of Jacob's Trouble, and on the contrary, it would be Christians who suffer the most at the hands of the antichrist. He was touched and considered this an unusual position for a Christian.

To help rebuild the Temple and to hasten the day of Christ is not self-serving to those who believe in a post-tribulation rapture. We see and know and understand the consequences of actions taken that will hasten the day of Christ, and *we pursue them anyway*.

Your Perfect Life in America is Not The Life of Millions of Christians

All three rapture views should consider this: tens of millions of Christians today live with a potential life disruption or sentence of death hanging over them for *merely* believing in Jesus. Over 380,000,000 Christians face persecution and discrimination world-wide (an irrational hate).

To this day Christian women and teen-aged girls in Nigeria, Egypt, and the Middle East are taken captive against their will to become "wives" of their Muslim captors. Christian husbands are sometimes slaughtered in front of their wives and children. Within recent memory in Turkey, two missionaries were tortured to death. Hindus attack Christians in India and burn their churches. Communist China jails and punishes Christians with impunity, bulldozing their church buildings. All irrational hate.

Do we need to review all that is going on in the world that grieves the heart of God? Can our hearts stand it? God weeps with us over grievous sin. How long will He wait to bring His will to bear on this planet? Are we personally in agony over the sins of the world and therefore want His kingdom to come as quickly as possible? Are our lives too cozy in America to worry about it?

Do we really pray that God's kingdom come and that His will be done on earth as it is in heaven and then turn away and ignore the chance to hasten the day of God and speed its coming?

Hastening the Day

"Hastening the day" should not be a threat to anyone who believes in a pre- or mid-tribulation rapture of the church (2 Peter 3:12). To hasten the day of Christ would mean the rapture would come sooner in either case. We could all agree and should all agree to help build the third Temple and to win the lost tribes of Israel to Christ.

Yet, there is a reluctance on the part of ordinary, everyday Christians to "hasten the day of Christ." Raising children, the call of everyday worries, and the necessities of life seem to trump everything else. The intent of God to bring His kingdom is seemingly on the back-burner for Christians, if it is on a burner at all. We are prosperous, not persecuted, and have great health care. We have planned out before us a glorious future on this present earth in detail. So, do we really care to hasten the Day of Christ?

The Temple and the Lost Tribes of Israel reveals where the lost tribes of Israel are now and how they are part of God's end-time prophecies. Also, through recent archaeology discoveries, the book uncovers the proper place for the Temple to be built—and it is not on the traditional Temple Mount. Recent archaeology has accidentally (and seemingly unknowingly) established the location of the former Temple south of the traditional Temple Mount and adjacent to the City of David.

At the end of *The Temple and the Lost Tribes of Israel*, there is a "Temple Memorial" for readers to sign. It calls on the president of the United States to encourage Israel to rebuild the Temple "on its site" (Ezra 2:68).

The Temple Memorial is modeled after the Blackstone Memorial that was signed by four hundred Christian leaders over one hundred and thirty years ago to be presented to President Harrison and subsequent presidents. It called for the president to encourage Zionism. Through human agency, motivated by the Word of God, and animated by the Spirit of God, this too hastened the day of Christ.

Through this Memorial and other Christian efforts, Israel eventually became a nation after almost 2,000 years of exile—see Lord Balfour's Christian support for Zionism in the Balfour Declaration (*Arthur James Balfour, First Earl of Balfour, K.G., O.M., F.R.S., ETC. 1848-1905*, Blanche E.C. Dugdale—his niece) and the help Chaplain William Hechler gave to Theodor Herzl (*The Politics of Christian Zionism, 1891-1948*, Paul C. Merkley).

For our purposes, we need several hundred thousand signatures to make the Temple Memorial viable. And I should add, **the Lord needs it** (Luke 19:31). If He needed a donkey to ride on and the disciples were to fetch it for Him and tell anyone who asked them "**the Lord needs it**," then we foresee the need for Christian involvement (Zechariah 6, "those who are far away") to rebuild the Temple. It must be in place before He returns—***the Lord needs it***.

Some Christians object that they *themselves* are a temple where the Holy Spirit dwells, which is of course true (1 Corinthians 6:19). It is, however, a spiritual, theological, and physical impossibility that the future antichrist comes to stand in the body of *their* temple! When Jesus foretold that the abomination of desolation would stand in God's Temple, He did not have in mind our bodies being *that* Temple of the Lord. This future structure is called God's Temple four times: *God's Temple* (2 Thessalonians 2:4), *the holy place* (Matthew 24:15), *the Temple of God* (Revelation 11:1) and *His sanctuary* (Daniel 8:11).

These two prophecies must be fulfilled: [1] A certain number of Israelis from *every* tribe must come to Christ, including from the ten lost Tribes of Israel. These tribes have not vanished from history, but they will not return to God and David their king until the last days (Hosea 3, Revelation 7). [2] Gentile Christians must help rebuild the Temple (Zechariah 6). Sitting on our hands is not an option—Zechariah declares **diligent action** is required (6:15). Until the fulfillment of these two prophecies—*Jesus will not return* and this we know is true by the authority of the Word of God itself.

This second one [#2] needed careful study to come to the conclusion that Christians should be interested in rebuilding the Temple. Zechariah 6:15—

> Those who are *far away* will come and help to build the temple of the LORD, and you will know that the LORD Almighty has sent me to you. This will happen if you ***diligently obey*** the LORD your God. (Emphasis added)

Isaiah helps us define the *far away*—

> You who are *far away*, hear what I have done; *you who are near*, acknowledge my power! (Isaiah 33:13, emphasis added)

Here Isaiah defines the *far away* as Gentiles as opposed to *you who are near* meaning the Jews. Luke tells us that God sent Paul *far away* to the Gentiles (Acts 22:21), and Paul tells his Greek converts—

> Remember that at that time you were separate from Christ, excluded from citizenship in Israel and foreigners to the covenants of the promise, without hope and without God in the world. But now in Christ Jesus you who were once *far away*

have been brought *near* by the blood of Christ. (Ephesians 2:12,13, emphasis added)

He came and preached peace to you who were *far away* and peace to those who were *near*. (Ephesians 2:17, emphasis added—used of Gentiles and Jews)

The Temple and the Lost Tribes of Israel argues that sitting on our hands is not a Christian response to Zechariah's call for diligent action. However, the church has declared over and over again that "God said it; I believe it; and that settles it!" perhaps unintentionally implying that there was nothing for us to do beyond mental assent. Unfortunately, for whatever reason, we have come to believe God will do *everything* and our participation is not required. We have become mere bystanders and observers, and we are content that way.

Contrary to this attitude, notice the acts of a not-very-righteous king of northern Israel. Jehu was commissioned by God to destroy the house of Ahab, and later he killed Joram the son of Ahab outside Jezreel. At that time, he recalled that the LORD had made a specific prophecy that Ahab would pay for the murder of Naboth on that very same plot of ground in Jezreel that belonged to Naboth (2 Kings 9:24-26).

In the original incident, Ahab had killed Naboth, and Elisha had subsequently pronounced God's judgment on the house of Ahab. In an amazing, shocking turn of events, Ahab humbled himself, tore his clothes, lay in sackcloth, and went about meekly (1 Kings 21:27-29). Because of this repentance, Elisha was told that the LORD would not bring about the family disaster in Ahab's time, but rather in the days of his son.

After killing Joram son of Ahab, Jehu reminded Bidkar of the prophecy and ordered him to pick up the body and to dump it on the field where Naboth had been killed. Thus, Jehu ensured the accomplishment of the word of the Lord given through Elisha. His actions partnered with the Lord to fulfill the word of the Lord.

Of course, the Lord could have fulfilled His word a different way, and we are reminded in this case of the words of Mordecai to Esther,

> For if you remain silent at this time, relief and deliverance for the Jews will arise from another place, but you and your father's family will perish. And who knows but that you have come to a royal position for such a time as this? (Esther 4:14)

The opportunity for Jehu to fulfill this prophecy was granted to him, and he availed himself of that opportunity. Our opportunities present themselves to us in a similar way.

We observed in *The Temple and the Lost Tribes of Israel* that Columbus himself felt it a privilege to be allowed partnership with God in his endeavors to win the islands of the sea for Christ (yes, that Columbus). He knew and acted on the fact that Christians should work for Christ to hasten His coming. Columbus knew that God's promises would prevail, but also saw that God afforded us the privilege to partner with Him to achieve the end that He guarantees. Columbus was an avid Bible student—he even acknowledged his salvation to Queen Isabella and King Ferdinand in very Protestant terms! (*The Libro de las Profecías of Christopher Columbus*, August Kling and Delno C. West).

The Scriptures are full of predictions about the return of Israel's exiled tribes in both the New and Old Testaments. We don't study it because of the perverse message of some of the cults that claim to be "the lost Tribes of Israel." *The Temple and the Lost Tribes of Israel* explores the claims of the Pashtuns of Afghanistan to be those tribes. The British knew about this more than 200 years ago, but the claim can be traced in Arabic literature even further back to the 9th century AD. The best thing about this is that the Afghans themselves claim to be those tribes and have many customs that favor an Israeli origin. As the Jews of Afghanistan made their way back to the newly formed State of Israel, they corroborated this claim of the Pashtuns to be sons of Israel.

The Temple and the Lost Tribes of Israel also traces the circuit Nehemiah's choirs took around the (newly identified) walls and towers of Jerusalem, which in turn yielded new insights into the Word of God and helped to locate the ancient Temple's position. Also, recent archaeological discoveries in the old City of David unintentionally make the case that the Temple was not on the traditional Temple Mount.

In reality, the traditional Temple Mount answers Josephus's description of the Roman fort Antonia: its size—a city within a city for size (big enough for 12,000 soldiers—a first century Roman legion), rectangular shape, elevation "like a tower," and its right and left gates—the Iron Gate (mentioned in Acts 12:10), and the Golden Gate. These two gates are in the right locations for a first century Roman fort—one third of the way down the long sides of the rectangle. The fort also had a rock-cut ditch that divided it from the hill to its north—precisely as we find at the traditional Mount.

The ramps on the south side of the traditional Mount, leading to the outside wall and facing south (down toward where we put the Temple) match Josephus's description of the fort's ramps at the Double and Triple Gates on the south wall of the traditional Temple Mount. A secret tunnel that Herod built on the south side of fort Antonia (which led down to the Temple) was found by Captain Warren of the Royal Engineers in 1867 and rediscovered by the Israelis in the 1970s under the south wall of the traditional Mount —built with Herodian style ashlars.

Due to traditional views of the Mount, these were not recognized as Josephus's ramps on the south side of the Roman fort nor was the secret tunnel recognized as Herod's secret tunnel. On the other hand, there is no secret tunnel nor are there Roman ramps on the north side of the traditional Mount.

The traditional Temple Mount itself does not answer to Josephus's description of the Temple, nor does it match the Mishnah or the Talmud's description. However, the terrain and geographical features described by Josephus that exist south of the Mount match his description and also match the Talmud's description of the Temple platform. *The Temple and the Lost Tribes of Israel* elaborates this more fully.

In 2015, the Israel Antiquities Authority (IAA) announced that they had found the long-lost, Greek fort Akra. It is south of the traditional Mount, found underneath the Givati parking lot next to the City of David. Archaeologists and historians had speculated about the Akra's whereabouts for centuries. What is interesting is that Nehemiah, Josephus, the Maccabees, and Aristeas all say the Akra abutted or was next to the Temple. Several of these witnesses say it was on the **north** side of the Temple and overlooked it. Where the IAA found the Akra is precisely next door to where we position the Temple and includes a very high perch that overlooks the **north** side of where we locate the Temple.

The recent discovery of the Greek fort Akra shows it was not on the north side of the traditional Temple Mount, nor does it overlook it—it is south of the traditional Mount and much lower than the Mount. But it does overlook and butt up against where we put the Temple on its north side, and this is corroborated by several other finds that we list in *The Temple and the Lost Tribes of Israel*.

Also corroborating the discoveries and observations above, my daughter and I identified the walls and towers that Uzziah built and the route Nehemiah's choirs used to walk around and dedicate Jerusalem's rebuilt walls from Nehemiah chapters 3 and 12 and also 2 Chronicles 25 & 26. The measurements between the gates and towers of the city are recorded for us in the Scriptures (400 cubits and 1000 cubits) and these match the detailed and marvelous map work of archaeologists Bliss and Dickie from the 1890s in the southwest corner of old Jerusalem.

Working for the Palestine Exploration Fund (the PEF), they uncovered these walls and towers, they drew very accurate maps, but it escaped their notice at that time how these fit into the narrative of the Scriptures. Yet, their great work changes how we look at the landscape of old of Jerusalem and helps fit together the puzzle of where the Temple used to be located. The Temple can now be built on its correct site without the threat of WWIII.

If you shrink back from Christian interest in rebuilding the Temple and think it odd, or even heresy—solve this riddle: Where does the Old Testament predict the mystery of the *first* and the *last* names of the Messiah? [Did you know the Messiah had a last name?] It is definitely there. If you were unaware of this, chapter 12 of *The Temple and the Lost Tribes of Israel* discusses this wonder in detail. And in this mystery, we find the Messiah's name woven into the story of restoring the Temple with Gentile Christian help (see Zechariah 6:9-15 and Jeremiah 23:6).

In a real way, it is a story for Christian evangelism. When we come and help build the Temple, the people of Israel will start to believe Zechariah and Jeremiah's prediction of the name of the Messiah.

You can see from my argument in favor of the post-tribulation rapture that the return of Christ is not imminent, and His return could not be realized until at least these two prophecies are brought to fulfillment. (See our *Post Script* for an exciting third prophecy that we cannot influence, but which must be fulfilled.)

Notice Jesus' requirement for world-wide evangelism before His return is already completed (or is almost complete), and this through the power of the Holy Spirit and by the actions of countless ambassadors for Christ. Remote areas of the earth were already reached in centuries past to include Africa, China,

Nepal, Socotra off the Horn of Africa, Madagascar, Burma, India, Afghanistan, Java, Japan, et cetera.

These twin prophecies about the Temple and winning to Christ some from *all* the tribes of Israel should appeal to the pre-tribulation, mid-tribulation, and post-tribulation churches as a matter of **obedience**—even if the first two don't believe in a post-tribulation rapture. To **obey** is better than sacrifice.

So, this is my manifesto to the Bible-believing church, whether holding a pre-tribulation view, a mid-tribulation view, or a post-tribulation view:

Let Us Join Together to Hasten the Day of Christ.

Join the evangelization of the Lost Tribes of Israel and join together to rebuild the Temple "on its site."

> Pray for the peace of Jerusalem...For the sake of the house of the LORD our God, I will seek your prosperity. (Psalm 122:6 & 9)

Post Script

There is a third prophecy that we cannot influence but still needs to occur. Thanks to the efforts of Dan Gibson, an important fact about Islam has been uncovered. Through decades of research, Dan has found that for the first one hundred years of Islam, the direction of prayer for Muslims was originally towards Petra in Jordan, not towards Mecca in Saudi Arabia (*Early Islamic Qiblas: A survey of mosques built between 1AH/622 C.E. and 263 AH/876 C.E.*).

He has a very compelling case. Even Muslim archaeologists have admitted to Dan that there are no artifacts nor is there any archaeological evidence that shows early Islam was in Mecca. Petra, in southern Jordan, on the other hand, matches the description and details of early Islamic history very well. Dan found that the ruins of early mosques all have their prayer wall (their qiblas) facing Petra with a remarkable degree of accuracy.

That brings us to a prophecy about the return of Christ that makes little sense at the moment. The context is the end-times:

> All the stars of the heavens will be dissolved and the sky rolled up like a scroll; all the starry host will fall ... My sword has drunk its fill in the heavens; see, it descends in judgment on Edom, the people I have totally destroyed. The sword of the LORD is bathed in blood, ...For the LORD has a sacrifice in Bozrah and a great slaughter in Edom. (Isaiah 34:4-6. **Bozrah**, the ancient capital of Edom, and Petra, its principal stronghold.)

But why will Christ be angry at the practically empty desert of southern Jordan? The area is almost uninhabited today. How and why might a great slaughter occur there in the fury of His wrath at His return? Of the day of God's vengeance Isaiah also writes:

> Who is this coming from Edom,
> from **Bozrah**, with his garments stained crimson?
> Who is this robed in splendor, striding forth in the greatness of his strength?
> 'It is I, speaking in righteousness,
> mighty to save.'
> Why are your garments red,
> like those of one treading the winepress?
> 'I have trodden the **winepress** alone;
> from the nations no one was with me.
> I trampled them in my anger
> and trod them down in my wrath;
> their blood spattered my garments,
> and stained all my clothing.' (Isaiah 63:1-3, emphasis added)

This reminds us of the coming of Christ in Revelation 19:13,15:

> He is dressed in a robe dipped in blood, and his name is the Word of God. Out of his mouth comes a sharp sword with which to strike down the nations. 'He will rule them with an iron scepter.' He treads the **winepress** of the fury of the wrath of God Almighty. (Emphasis added)

Two things could possibly line up for this to take place, but the first of these would certainly be necessary. [1] Large numbers of people completely hostile to Jews and Christians would have to move to southern Jordan to warrant the great wrath of Jesus. This alone would set up the fulfillment of the prophecy.

Also, this second item could possibly explain why so many would move there: [2] A huge earthquake would flatten Mecca in Saudi Arabia—thereby embarrassing the Saudis who are supposed to be the guardians of the two cities of the faithful, Mecca and Medina. (Mecca sits on top of a major fault line. A geologist friend of mine told me the Saudis requested his help with this pressing problem—not that he could stop an earthquake, but it shows their great concern were this to happen.)

If this earthquake becomes a reality, Muslims would presume that their god displayed his anger at the Saudi family for their secret (but still-well-known) liberalism. Presently, the Saudi royal family pays the Wahabi (fundamentalist) clerics to look the other way and concentrate on other things besides them. In the future, this liberalism might also include a treaty of peace with Israel. (As of this writing, the Abrahamic Peace Accords have not yet extended to Saudi Arabia—April 2025.) To save face for Islam, Gibson's research on Petra would be embraced.

Islam is hugely hostile to Israel and to the followers of Christ. It is baked into their theology that the end-times cannot happen until every single Jew in the *world* is killed. Though both Jews and Christians are called the "People of the Book" and therefore protected under humiliating "Dhimmi laws," in practice, this was never adhered to in Islamic history, and the Jews and Christians were pillaged over and over (see Bat Ye'or cited above).

Humiliation and plundering, high taxation and false accusations, gang rape and forced conversions, forced 'marriages' and wife stealing, mass death and enslavement, beatings and stoning, helplessness under the law and dispossession of property (to include money and jewelry, lands, houses, synagogues, businesses, and church buildings), exile and impaling victims, crucifixions and breaking treaties, and many other predations down through history perpetuated against Jews and Christians always trumped their so-called "Dhimmi" protections for unbelievers, the "People of the Book." The West is blissfully unaware of this history and more often than not would be afraid to mention it if they knew it. Publishers demand that authors tone down their rhetoric and self-censor when it comes to this subject.

For sense to be made of Isaiah's prophecies, large numbers of hostile people must move to southern Jordan and be involved with things that call down the particular wrath of God at the second coming of Jesus. I believe Muslims will flock there in large numbers when Mecca is flattened and Gibson's work becomes well-known. Infrastructure must be built up in order for this to be fulfilled—and that takes time.

In the end-times, southern Jordan will earn the **wrath** of God in spades—guaranteed. Isaiah's prophecy was a bit disconcerting and inexplicable when we tried to understand it before. Dan Gibson's work came like a thunderbolt out of the blue to explain these passages in Isaiah. Now it makes perfect sense.

May the God of Peace give you peace as you study these things. Amen.

www.ingramcontent.com/pod-product-compliance
Lightning Source LLC
Chambersburg PA
CBHW071731090426
42738CB00011B/2452